BALL CRAZY

BALL CRAZY

Confessions of a Dad-Coach

Hal Jacobs

(FOR NOW)

an imprint of everthemore books

This book is for Alicia, Daniel & Henry.

Copyright ©2010 by Hal Jacobs
All Rights Reserved for the Author

Published by
FOR NOW
an imprint of everthemore books
www.everthemorebooks.com
484-C Moreland Ave NE
Atlanta, Georgia 30307

ISBN-13 978-0-9743877-3-4

ISBN-10 0-974-38773-8

Like so much else between fathers and sons, playing catch was tender and tense at the same time.... Baseball is fathers and sons playing catch, lazy and murderous, wild and controlled, the profound archaic song of birth, growth, age, and death. This diamond encloses what we are.

>Donald Hall, *Fathers Playing Catch with Sons: Essays on Sport*, North Point Press, 1984.

- 1 -

It's Friday evening at a youth baseball complex in Tyrone, Georgia. Dusk has settled into the grass and trees beyond the outfield fence, turning them into something resembling quiet woodlands. But the baseball diamond is as brightly lit as an operating room.

At the moment, our team of twelve-year-olds, the Druid Hills Bulls, are getting waxed. We're down 10-0 in the last inning. The team we're facing is so well-coached and so all-around good—the word is that they won some world series out West last year—that it feels more clinical than your typical 10-0 beat down. It might hurt more in the morning.

Then it starts to get interesting.

An out here, a few seeing-eye hits there, a walk, another out, and bases are loaded with two outs. It's time for my son, Henry, to step into the batter's box.

Moments like this are the hardest. There's nothing on the line—this is just another Friday night in another weekend tournament. But for some crazy reason, to at least one person watching this game, it feels like everything is on the line.

I should start walking away, down the right field line, away from the blinding whiteness of home plate. I should call someone on my cell phone, someone who thinks there are more important things in life than baseball, and make plans to do something tomorrow that has nothing to do with baseball.

I should do anything but what I am doing, gripping the chainlink fence and praying for a miracle.

Please, God, please. . . grant him a hit.

I don't want it for me. I want it for him. I want my son to be happy.

Henry cocks his bat. Damp locks of hair poke out from his dirty batting helmet. He's sweaty from catching behind the plate the whole game and from throwing himself around like a rag doll while trying to block curve balls in the dirt. His cheeks and stomach still carry a hint of that adolescent softness that will melt away in another year. At this moment, everything is pure and anything is possible.

In my mind, I can already see his swing and the metal bat meeting the red-seamed ball at that perfect sweet spot, the little white orb disappearing like a shooting star over the outfield fence. I can see this without the first pitch even being thrown, which makes me feel like I'm hallucinating.

The pitcher winds up and throws a fastball down the middle of the plate.

Henry watches it.

"Strike!" yells the umpire, pumping his fist with the conviction of a man who knows that in a few more minutes he'll be sitting in a camp chair beside his car in the parking lot and cracking open a cold one from the cooler.

The finality of the ball slamming into the catcher's mitt—instead of leaping off Henry's bat—is a little disorienting to me. What just happened? I look around to see if anyone else just noticed that he didn't swing at the ball. His teammates in the dugout beside me are experiencing a range of emotions: the next two batters have their helmets on and want a chance to hit; the others are squirming on the bench, looking forward to the game being over so they can start the next adventure.

Some fathers I know would take it personally that their kid didn't swing at that pitch. I'm not that bad. But I am wracking my brain for the reason why he wouldn't offer at a perfectly grooved fastball. Is he still smarting from his last at bat, when he swung at a first-pitch curve ball and grounded weakly to shortstop? Or did the Skipper give him the take sign from third base?

My mouth feels rusty, like I've been sucking on a dirty penny. The buzzing of the overhead lights grows louder, raspier. My mistake was in thinking that I could pray to one baseball god and get some satisfaction. There are many baseball gods—a true polytheism of deities that love to screw with us.

My vision of a ball ascending into the dusky sky is now replaced by the hot pain of doubt and fear. A strikeout to end the game would hurt bad. The absence of all hope. Hell.

Baseball can be such a cruel game.

Henry steps out of the batter's box, nods as he gets his sign from the Skipper, takes a deep breath, and digs back in. He looks a little tight up there. I once heard Archie Manning say it was harder for him to watch his young sons play football than to play the game himself. I can relate to that, even if the closest I've come to professional sports is five seats behind the visitor's dugout at Turner Field.

Strike two. Damn.... A curve that starts inside and then dies on the outer part of the plate. I wish I could step back and admire the finesse of this pitcher. I'm sure some parent on the other side is feeling very satisfied at the moment. But let's face it. My kid just fell into a deep hole. I can see him, but I can't help him.

I can still remember those days before my addiction made a 0-2 pitch feel like a punch to the gut. Five years ago, when we enrolled in organized youth baseball, I never ever thought I would become one of those dads with a baseball problem. I didn't grow up playing organized ball. I was a sandlot kid whose parents never had a clue what I did for ten hours every day. I never counted down the days until my sons, Henry and his older brother, could compete. My wife and I never wanted to be among those parents who lined up bookings for their children like a tour manager.

But after tonight's game, we have a doubleheader scheduled for tomorrow, then a Sunday game to be determined, then weeknight practices, followed by another tournament that starts next weekend, then two more weeks of this before we enter the PONY district tournament at the end of the month. It's a forced march in which our normal lives are subordinated to the needs of the team.

The next pitch is a changeup in the dirt. Henry lays off it. Thank God. With a 1-2 count, Henry knows his job is to protect the plate. And if he's forgotten, he's got two or three parents yelling at him from the stands.

It's been a long night for them—and a long two weeks. Ever since Memorial Day weekend, when the Bulls hit the road to play in tournaments, we've been buoying the hopes of other teams, while sinking lower and lower in our own estimation. Granted, we're inexperienced. Unlike most travel teams that hit the road around Valentine's Day and go strong up to Halloween, our team of "all stars" is comprised of players from five different teams at the little park where we wrapped up our spring PONY recreational season.

Our lifespan is about as long as one of the cicadas that rasps out from the trees beyond the outfield. We'll play in four or five of these travel-ball tournaments, then take our chances in the the PONY qualifiers that lead to the PONY World Series in mid-August.

According to the Skipper's plan, these travel-ball tournaments will hone our skills and confidence. But lately we resemble more of a butter knife than a steel cutting edge.

Last weekend, when the "team sucked so bad," according to one of the dads, it was because a starting pitcher, two starting catchers, and a starting middle infielder were on vacation. To make matters worse, two of the fathers who went AWOL were assistant dad-coaches. And one of those father-son combinations was Henry and me. It goes without saying that a real "baseball man" would never go on a camping trip with his family until after the baseball season.

So this week, Henry and I have worked hard to regain the confidence of our pack. The first day back we were sniffed at and growled at (one dad asked if I was going on any more vacations this month), but by last night's practice we had almost stopped feeling like outcasts.

By the way, youth baseball, like wolf packs and the military, has an extremely rigid social structure. The need for this isn't so obvious until you find yourself in a do-or-die situation: a situation that calls for quick, decisive action, either on the field or immediately after the game in deciding which fastfood restaurant the team should invade.

The alpha dad-coach on our team is the Skipper, manager and third-base coach. He's a baseball man who earned his stripes by playing in the same little neighborhood park where he has coached all three of his sons and by having a pitching career that extended to a few years on the mound at Georgia Tech. My appointment as dad-coach came from the Skipper ("It'll be fun—and twelve is absolutely the best age for coaching boys' baseball"). My main qualifications are (1) I have a son who, without any help from me, can throw strikes and block curve balls in the dirt; and (2) my flexible work schedule allows me to structure my entire life around The Team.

Restoring father and son back into everyone's good graces is yet another reason why a hit right now would be so sweet.

Here comes the next pitch. A good one—for the pitcher—not Henry. Low and on the outside part of the plate. Too close to take. Henry loads his bat and swings.

He gets good composite metal on the ball—I hear a sharp, satisfying ring—followed by cheers and yells from the stands and dugout.

The groundball shoots to the right side of the infield. For a moment it looks like it might get into right field and score two runs. Henry is tearing up the ground between home plate and first. But the first baseman takes a few steps to his right, stays down on the ball as it disappears into the leather webbing of his glove, then steps on first before Henry arrives in a fury of arms and legs.

Ball game.

- 2 -

MY ADOPTED FATHER and grandfather, both of them long-distance truck drivers, stand before me in the middle of the living room. In the background, an afternoon baseball game plays on the black-and-white TV. It's a long-ago moment from my childhood that for some reason has never faded. I am four or five years old and listening closely to their conversation about somebody named Mickey. Finally, even though I'm not supposed to interrupt grownups, I can't stand it any longer.

"Are you talking about Mickey Mouse?"

They stop in mid-sentence. My father, a no-nonsense ex-Navy man whose arms, legs and chest are filled with tattoos that range from a lion's head to a full-figured swimsuit girl, gives me a hard look for interrupting. Or for being a wise ass. Because he spends most of his week on the road, he doesn't know if I'm pulling his leg or not.

My grandfather, who will retire soon from truck driving to spend most of his days at the Paxton Lounge, located in a nearby shopping center, gives me a big grin with the gleaming white dentures set in his tanned, wrinked face. "No, Mickey Mantle. The baseball player."

What's so strange is that, over forty years later, these are the only words I can remember between myself and my adopted father, who died when I was eight, or my grandfather, who drank himself out of our lives. I never played catch with either of them and besides this conversation, don't remember ever talking about baseball.

A few years later, I discovered baseball by myself at the little park near our house. It was sandlot baseball where the trees on the field outnumbered the players. But until I was twelve years old it was the most important thing in my life.

That's all to say, the version of baseball I grew up with bears absolutely no resemblance to the organized game that my sons play.

- 3 -

THE FIRST GAME of today's doubleheader starts at noon, but my stomach has been churning since the first cup of coffee, around 7 a.m. Henry takes the mound for game one. And that always makes me crazy.

A few years ago, my older son, Daniel, lay in the hospital with a ruptured appendix. It was the first brush with a medical emergency involving our children that my wife and I had experienced. As I was driving from the hospital after spending a sleepless night on the too-small sofa in the hospital room, I felt impatient with the world around me, particularly those commuters driving to work and sipping travel mugs without a care in the world.

On days when Henry takes the mound, it's not quite a matter of life or death. But it is gut-wrenching in a way that feels primitive and makes me identify a bit with fathers like Abraham on the day he led his son to that big rock in the desert, and Daedulus on the day he took his son flying.

On pitching days, it's almost like I'm experiencing phantom limb syndrome—and Henry is the missing limb. Before the game and especially when he's on the mound, it's as if we're attached in some strange neural way. It's excruciating, and gives "living through your child" a whole new dimension.

I'm not sure if Henry realizes how badly this team needs a win. It's a subject I would never bring up with him before the game. After years of hit-and-mostly-miss results, I now avoid the big pre-game motivational speech from dad that not only prepares him mentally and emotionally for the game, but also inspires him to become a leader among men and a better citizen in our democratic way of life. Looking back, I believe these speeches owe a lot to Frank Capra movies and were more for my benefit than his.

These days I pick my moments more carefully. On today's forty-minute drive south on I-75 to the Tyrone, Ga., ballpark, I say nothing as we cruise and listen to classic rock on the radio, then turn into the park's gravel driveway, cruising past the woman camped out at a portable card table collecting $5 from everyone but players and coaches.

Finally I turn down the radio and pat his knee. "Keep the ball down and you'll be fine. As long as you get the ball down, they'll hit groundballs and our infield will take care of them."

Henry nods, then cranks up the music to hear the rest of the Jimi Hendrix solo.

After three innings, the score is tied 2-2. Henry is throwing strikes, and so is the other pitcher. The game is cruising along. Our teams look evenly matched. The only big difference, at this point, is that their players chatter with the kind of Deep South accents you find about an hour drive outside of Atlanta.

"Hey!" calls out the little second baseman, quickly followed up by "Oh!" from the first baseman. They draw out the vowels so the words run into each other. "Hey . . . oh . . . ." Again and again. "Hey . . . oh . . . ."

"Hey batter batter batter . . . . MISS!"

"Rip-rip . . . . Rip-rip . . . . Rip-rip . . . . Rip-rip . . . . Rip-rip . . . ."

"He don't want it!"

But if he swings and misses: "Dugout time!"

When one of our players tries to retaliate with his own halfhearted chant, one of his teammates tells him to shut up.

We have a little rally going in the bottom of the third, runners on first and second, no outs, when something happens that changes everything.

Our runner on second gets his primary lead, about three steps off the bag, when the pitcher whirls towards second. Naturally, our runner puts his head down and starts back to the bag. At the same time, both the shortstop and second baseman start running towards the bag, diving on the ground, while behind them, the centerfielder starts running frantically, then stumbles. Everyone else on the field and in their dugout is shouting, "Git the ball!"

Naturally, our base runner bolts for third base. But in his haste, he doesn't happen to notice the Skipper, standing behind third base, motioning him to go back to second. And before he can race halfway to third, the pitcher walks up to him and tags him out.

The old hidden ball trick.

Our poor guy jogs off the field, back to the dugout, looking like an accident victim. Meanwhile, the players and coaches on the other team are laughing and celebrating like they just pulled a winning lottery ticket.

I've never seen anything like this in youth baseball before. It seems like an incredibly mean stunt to pull on a twelve year old. I can't believe it.

I know trickery and deception are part of the game. But the ensuing celebration by the players on the field—and the coaches in the dugout—is unbelievable. I'm feeling the same kind of road rage I'd feel if some butthead cut me off on the interstate while text messaging.

That's how things get crazy. Something like this happens to your child, and suddenly you find yourself starring on page B3 of the metro section and looking for legal advice. Now the game is personal. And the only way we can get satisfaction is by smoting our enemy.

So when Henry takes the mound in the fourth inning, the score still tied, I want him to deliver some Old Testament-style retribution on the tribe of our twelve-year-old foes and their elders.

Fortunately, Henry isn't as worked up as I am. The Skipper didn't make a big deal about ball trick, so that probably helped. Henry retires the side, three up, three down. We, too, go quietly in the bottom of the inning. I'm still steaming.

In the fifth inning, Henry gives up a few hits to let them take a 3-2 lead. One of our dads approaches me in the dugout. "He's thrown seventy pitches," he says, holding up a little electronic scorebook.

As much as I know this dad's heart is in the right place and he's trying to be helpful, I also know he wants to get his son, our substitute right fielder—the same boy who got picked off second—into the game to pitch relief. He wants to give his kid a shot at redemption. I'd do the same thing in his shoes.

But frankly, at this point, I think Henry is the horse we should be riding—and seventy pitches is still within the realm of his well-being. Anyway, even though he's my flesh and blood, it's the Skipper's call, and I know where he stands on the subject of pitch counts: unless a pitcher's arm starts screaming, he needs to stay out there until he can smell the barn.

In the bottom of the fifth, we're up to bat. We've got another rally going, this time with two runners on, no outs. From the coach's box at third, the Skipper calls out so everyone can hear him loud and clear: "If they put their clown noses on and start rolling around in the dirt, don't go anywhere!"

Our players start grinning.

The smallest kid on the team, our little ball-hawk in centerfield, drives a 3-2 pitch to the gap in right centerfield. We tie up the game, 3-3.

The next batter, our speedy second baseman, lays a perfect bunt down the third base line—you could not roll the ball any better with your hand—and the pitcher throws it away down the first base line.

Good guys 5, sneaky guys 3.

When the Bambino comes up to bat next—Coach Sam and I have privately nicknamed him this because of his eerie resemblance to a young Babe Ruth and his occasional fence-clearing blasts—I notice that his mother, wearing an all-white flowing dress, walks in the clearing just outside the left field fence.

"The lady in white," Coach Sam murmurs.

The Bambino strikes out. When he lumbers back into the dugout, he gripes that the Skipper gave him the take sign on the first pitch.

It's the sixth inning. I'm counting Henry's pitches now. It only takes him two pitches to get a groundball out. Four more pitches for an easy fly ball. Then a kid fouls off a few before he strikes out. His pitch count is up to 84.

Behind me, the dad with the count gizmo is slowly shaking his head.

When Henry comes into the dugout, his face flushed like a strawberry, the Skipper asks him how his arm feels. Henry nods okay.

But when he glances at me standing at the other end of the dugout, I have to look away. I can tell how worn out he is, how close he is to the breaking point and how he's trying to tough it out. The last thing he needs to see right now is how much I know.

Or how proud I am. It's nearly 100 degrees on the clay infield, yet he wants to finish what he started. He also knows that when the Skipper asks how his arm feels, he's supposed to nod okay. That's what tough guys do.

He goes back to the mound for the last inning. Six pitches later, we get the final out and win the game.

When I put my arm around him afterwards, his skin is steaming hot through the jersey. I tell him it's the best game he's ever pitched.

The other parents come up to him with a steady outpouring of thanks. He quietly accepts their praise. I have no idea what he's thinking, or if he's thinking at all. He's been at the center of our world—ten players and twenty or so parents, siblings, grandparents— for nearly the last two hours. Last night his at-bat ended the game and he walked away in tears. Eighteen hours later, he's the king of the hill.

- 4 -

I CAN DISTINCTLY remember the first neighborhood sandlot baseball game I played in. I was nine years old. It was the spring after my father's death. The park in our working-class neighborhood consisted of two wooded, undeveloped city blocks. From my driveway, it was only four houses to the street corner, then the park. But it was strictly off-limits.

My mother had her reasons. She was an avid reader of those "official detective" magazines, so she was predisposed to thinking that either she or her children would eventually wind up in the hands of a sociopathic drifter. Also, I was small for my age and attended a Catholic school with my two sisters. In the afternoon we walked home from the bus stop in our plaid uniforms. I was the only male in the neighborhood, as far as I could tell, who wore a tie to work. With all this counting against me, it probably didn't matter that I was the only child in the neighborhood who was adopted at birth and had no idea who his real mother or father was.

A few other reasons stood out. Adults never frequented the park except for the men who parked their cars by the road for lunch breaks—or whatever else they did (sometimes we found seamy evidence). The teenagers who played football and baseball in the park—and sometimes drove their muscle cars into the park to spin donuts—cursed like longshoremen. Most of them attended Robert E. Lee High School, where one of their classmates, Ronnie Van Zant, was in a band that would soon be renamed for gym teacher Leonard Skinner. They were an exotic tribe to me, who only observed them from a safe distance. Their younger brothers and I would eye each other from time to time, but that was about it.

On the day I make my rookie appearance at the park, the baseball gods were watching out for me. No doubt the gods had glimpsed me playing catch for hours by myself in the driveway near the front door. With the glove I got from the S&H Green Stamps showroom near our house, I learned to catch by using the brick side of our front stoop that faced the driveway. By throwing a hard rubber ball downward against the wall, I could snag grounders. By throwing the ball so it hit the concrete driveway first, I worked on line drives and pop ups. The mortar between the bricks loosened and turned to powder as I kept count, trying to break previous world records of my own setting. The punishment for missing a ball was crawling through the neighbor's stickly bushes to find it.

I also read every boy's book on baseball at the public library. My favorite was about the boy who practiced hitting by rolling balls off the roof of his barn until he could make contact with anything thrown at him, although for some reason he could only foul things off until finally drawing a walk. Eventually, he wins the big game by, surprise!, hitting one fair for the first time in his life. At least that's how I remember it.

On this afternoon, my little sister and I were returning on foot from the little neighborhood store that was only a few blocks away from the park. In the months following my father's death at the age of forty-two, our house had gone dark. Except for a steady stream of Patsy Cline and Jim Reeves records playing on the new Montgomery Wards stereo console, the house was quiet as well. The roots of our little nuclear family only extended to my grandfather, and it was a special event whenever he dropped by. Today he had slipped me and my sister a dollar, and told us to spend it all on candy.

The park didn't have a name. It says something about the neighborhood that no one cared enough to erect a sign—or signs didn't last for long. Longleaf pines dropped fat cones and layers of long brown needles on the grass. Tall "Welcome to Florida" palm trees lined the edge of the two streets that separated the park in half.

As we approached the park, I studied the dozen or so boys scattered across the field until the diamond snapped into focus. The pitcher throwing overhanded, but not hard, from a dirt patch in the middle of the grassy field. The boy with a bat standing over a glove lying on the ground—home plate. Angled to the right, in front of a palm tree, was another dirt patch. First base. Second base was near a stand of crepe myrtles, and third was a pine tree jutting out from other pines.

A boy was standing amid trees in what must have been left field, a few others guarded center field, and right field was the road we were walking down. About ten or twelve boys all together. Mixed in were a few boys that looked to be my age. That caused my heart to beat faster. So they let smaller boys play.

I stopped next to some pine trees that were a safe distance from the home plate area. My sister stopped munching on the candy necklace in her mouth long enough to say, "What are you doing?"

"I want to watch the game."

"We're going to get in trouble."

"I don't care."

"I'm going to tell."

"Go ahead."

I pretended she wasn't there, although I needed her there. I pretended that I was just killing time, that I had nothing better to do. Inside, I was burning up. I wanted to be the one running through the trees in left field to catch a fly ball. I wanted to be the one hitting the ball hard up the middle, just missing the crepe myrtle trees, and racing to first. I didn't want to be the one that the other boys were calling a new word that I had never heard before.

What happened next was the miracle I was waiting for. My gift from the baseball gods. The ball bounced away from the boy who was playing catcher and bumped over the roots towards me and my sister.

No infielder making the final out in any World Series game ever needed a baseball more than I did at that moment. I picked it up, saw the catcher nod and hold out his glove towards me, then saw the pitcher beyond him, and threw the ball as far as I could, sailing it far and wide.

"Nice throw," somebody said, which I took to be a compliment, although it probably wasn't.

"We have to go home," said my sister.

Then I heard another voice. One of the big boys—my new hero—saying, "You want to play?"

"Sure."

"You can play left field."

Somebody tossed me a glove.

My sister looked at me in disbelief and betrayal.

"Go home," I said. "Tell them I'm playing baseball."

- 5 -

PITCHING A BASEBALL IS, to put it mildly, a torturous and self-destructive act. This is the opinion of the research director of the American Sports Medicine Institute, who explains why in these words: "Pitching is the fastest known motion in human bio-mechanics, the shoulder rotating at the rate of 7,200 degrees per second at its maximum, or the equivalent of 20 full revolutions per second. At the time of the ball's release, the forces acting on the shoulder are basically equivalent to the pitcher's body weight; they are akin to someone of similar size trying to yank his arm out of his shoulder socket."

As the father of a pitcher, when I hear something like this, I wonder: What the hell are we doing to our children?

I've read somewhere that pitching coach Rick Peterson wouldn't let his three sons pitch until they turned fifteen. Peterson tells a story of once throwing 200 pitches in a single game for his community college team, then pitching in relief the next day. Subsequently, a tendon in his throwing arm fell off the bone.

Geez....

I'm not one of those parents who thinks we need to spare Henry's arm now so he can be a million-dollar bonus baby one day. I gave up those illusions years ago (well, almost two years ago). I'm talking about saving his arm so that when he's my age he can throw batting practice to his children. Many of the older dad-coaches at our park can't even do that because of scar tissue from their Little League and high school playing days.

One problem for dads like me is that there is so much information out there that I don't know who to believe. Do you believe a former major leaguer who ripped a tendon in his pitching arm? Or do you believe dads from the park who've been down this road before and whose sons went on to pitch in high school and college? Or do you believe the orthopedists who are performing the kind of complicated elbow and shoulder operations on young pitchers that used to be reserved for adults?

"We really feel like what we are seeing, at least in our area of the country, is an awful lot of throwing over a four- or five-year period, as these kids move from Little League to high school, and some of the problems we are seeing in high school and early college can be linked back to what they were doing as eight- and nine-year-olds," said a family physician who practices sports medicine in Birmingham, Ala., at an annual meeting of the American Medical Society for Sports Medicine.

The same doctor recommends that a child eleven to twelve years old not throw more than seventy-five pitches in a game and rest for at least four days between outings. Throwing in the backyard or with a coach is good because it helps increase strength and flexibility. It's the hard, competitive throwing that leads to fatigue and injuries.

And then there's the whole "Should Children Throw Curveballs?" controversy. Dad-coaches can spend a whole night discussing the pros and cons of that one. Years ago I decided that Henry shouldn't throw curveballs. Instead, he worked on locating his fastball and developing a changeup. Our tall lefty, on the other hand, throws a loopy curve and a hard slider that his middle school coach taught him. He usually walks as many batters as he strikes out, but he's the only player on the team that has other coaches salivating when they watch him pitch.

Just for the record, USA Baseball, sponsor of the National Team and Olympic Team, surveyed 28 experienced orthopedic surgeons and baseball coaches about when a player should be allowed to start throwing breaking balls. At least fourteen years old was their recommendation for throwing curve balls in competition, and no sliders until the age of sixteen.

A year ago, we had our own brush with a pediatric orthopedist specialist. After Henry complained about his elbow hurting when he pitched, we took him to a local sports clinic.

The exam interview went something like this.

Specialist to Henry: "What happened?"

Henry: "My dad was my coach and he made me pitch too much."

Me: "Ha ha."

Awkward silence.

I refrained from pointing out to the doctor that THAT WAS MY LINE. I had used it a few days earlier, with Henry at my side, when a good friend asked me what was wrong with Henry's arm.

But it was true. I was one of his coaches for his spring recreational league team. Henry pitched the maximum innings allowed by the PONY Association, which was four innings in a game followed by forty hours of rest, with a maximum of ten innings per week. By almost all standards (except for Peterson's), that's a light pitching load, especially when you consider that a strike-throwing pitcher may sometimes throw fewer than ten pitches—all fastballs down the middle of the plate—in a single inning.

The problem is that when Henry wasn't pitching up to ten innings a week, he was catching behind the plate or playing shortstop. And on days he wasn't playing, he and I were tossing the ball in the front yard or on the sidelines of his brother's JV games.

The sports clinic X-ray revealed a slightly wider space of the soft tissue area between the bones in his right elbow compared to his left. Little League elbow it was.

The doctor said he was seeing this far too often. "He needs to stop pitching now. If he was mine, I wouldn't let him pitch again because once the high school coaches get a hold of him, they could care less what happens to his arm."

"What if he does want to pitch again?" I replied, a little too quickly.

The doctor didn't say it, but his manner indicated that he was also hearing way too much of this from parents as well.

"Take six months off from throwing a ball, then see how it feels."

On the car ride home, Henry and I talked over what this meant.

"The good thing is, we know what's going on," I said. "And nothing is hurt. We just need to take it easy."

So he wouldn't be pitching any more this spring, and he would be taking off the summer all star season as well.

For his part, Henry felt both disappointed and vindicated. For weeks he had been saying his arm was sore after he pitched. But I attributed this to growing pains and the soreness that is every pitcher's lot. Now he had solid right to say, "I told you so."

When we told other parents at the park about the diagnosis, I wasn't quite prepared for some of their reactions. While most people expressed concern and hope for a speedy recovery, quite a few of the parents, particularly the ex-high-school jocks and the mothers who had been through youth baseball before with older sons, looked skeptical.

In the words of one mom, "I respect your decision to keep Henry from pitching."

Then it dawned on me. To the veteran parents, I was giving my son a way out. Because pitching can be such a hard grind, both physically and emotionally, some boys will say anything to get off the mound.

One dad advised me the best way to work through a sore arm was to keep on pitching. "Pretty soon they forget all about their sore arms." Another dad suggested that I keep Advil cycling through Henry's system. "A little pain is a natural part of the game," he said.

When I mentioned the X-ray and the widening of the growth plates, I could tell that some of the dads thought this was my first mistake—taking my son to the doctor.

Pampering him.

So Henry stopped pitching for half a season in the spring of his eleventh year. He spent most of his time at first base—where he was able to chat with other players about why he couldn't pitch. He didn't make the combined eleven- and twelve-year-old all star team, even though most of his friends did. Over the course of the summer, we were regaled with stories about how great their team was.

The six months passed. In the fall, Henry began pitching again without any discomfort, though without the same velocity, which the other dads and players duly noted. But a few of the veteran dads seemed surprised to see him back on the mound at all.

One day the Skipper and I were talking about "good" and "bad" arm pain, with soreness being good and a screaming elbow being bad. He mentioned that he had bone chips floating around in his elbow from where he had chipped off the growth plate as a young pitcher.

"For most players," he said, "the only time they'll get to be a big sports star is when they're pitching here. Most of these guys won't survive the cut to make it as high school pitchers, and only a rare few will get a whiff of pitching on college team. So why not let them go as far as they can. After all, their memories will last a lifetime."

That almost made sense.

"So it's worth the arm pain in later years?" I asked. "And the arthritis that will probably kick in when you get older?"

He mulled this over for a moment. "Probably not."

- 6 -

My childhood baseball field only revealed itself to a chosen few. Occasionally, when riding by on the way to church, I would look out the back window and squint my eyes until I saw the fuzzy outlines of the park like I imagined everyone else did. To me, it was magical the way our field came to life when we stepped on it to play ball.

The big boys had their field on the other side of the road—that was the first place I had ever played. But that was months earlier. Now it was summer and I was hanging out with about a half-dozen boys my own age.

We stepped off the bases on our new field and laid down the ground rules. Right field was always closed, mostly because we never had enough players but also because of the trees. Left field was open to anyone who could drive a ball between the tall pines at second and third; a fly ball that crossed the two-lane asphalt road was a homerun.

The only problem with our layout stood behind the right-handed batter's box at home plate. A rogue palm tree, about twenty-five or thirty feet high, cursed that patch of bare dirt. The tree sucked foul tips out of the air. Not all the time, mind you, but just enough to lull us into complacency before snapping one up. We only had one ball at a time. Buying a new one could take days as we collected bottles to return at the store for a nickel apiece, doing yard work for neighbors, or stealing loose change from family members. Sad to say, I pried out every silver dime in my father's Mercury dime collection to pay for new baseballs.

When a ball landed in the ugly brown stubs of that tree, we cursed the batter and tree with everything we had. For years, that bastard tree symbolized everything in life that was big and unfair. We talked about sneaking out one night to cut it down, but like most things we talked about, no one ever followed through.

Years later, I wrote a fiction story about my sandlot days in which a telephone lineman, who has been working on utility poles near the park for weeks, finally drives his cherry-picker truck up to the tree. He rises up, then starts tossing down a seemingly never-ending supply of balls to the grateful boys.

- 7 -

"*How did Alexander Cartwright ever think of this game?*" asks our shortstop. He sits in the dugout and watches sweat drip from his nose to the hot concrete floor, where it quickly evaporates. We are losing the second game of a doubleheader, and nobody really cares.

"He must've been really bored," says the ball-hawk centerfielder.

This raises a good point. How did youth baseball evolve from sandlot games to weekend tournaments that require the logistics of a Special Forces operation?

The official Little League website points out that the first efforts to organize children's baseball games started in the 1880s, when professional clubs formed pre-teen leagues in New York City. At the time, only a decade or so after the setting of Scorcese's film *Gangs of New York*, the boroughs were flooded by new residents from overseas as well as the countryside. But the rural folks didn't bring baseball with them. Despite its agrarian feel, baseball was an urban, industrial game.

Historian Steven Gelber writes that baseball served as a kind of safety valve for urban pressures. (See the Notes section at the end of the book for information on sources used in this section). It reinforced city life and business organization. Players dealt with the same issues on the field as they found in the workplace— respect for obedience, responsibility, and a desire for achievement on both the individual and team level. So the game brought men "psychological harmony," which is probably something we hope our children get out of youth baseball these days. Maybe one day we'll even hear a mom scream out, in the heat of the moment, "Get some psychological harmony!"

There isn't much information available on these 1880s youth leagues. It would be interesting to know if they were aimed at working-class children or were an effort to reform the hordes of street urchins and pickpockets that stalked middle-class city dwellers. But since the youth leagues were closely affiliated with professional clubs, we can assume that professional baseball men organized the leagues instead of relying on dad-coaches in this pre-leisure-time era.

By the 1920s, baseball had become the universal language in streets, vacant fields and schoolyards. Babe Ruth learned to play the game at an orphanage. In fact, according to Leigh Montville in *The Big Bam*, Babe's batting instructor was Brother Matthias

Bouttlier, also Prefect of Discipline, who would hit towering fly balls (not a common sight in the dead-ball era) to the delight of the children. In 1925, the American Legion gave teenagers their first chance to play in national championship tournaments.

Ted Williams, who came of age in San Diego in the 1930s, starred in both high school and American Legion ball. In his adolescent years, however, before he was old enough to play organized baseball, he was lucky enough to live near a neighborhood park that had a playground instructor who was a former college player. As Ed Linn writes in *Hitter: The Life and Turmoils of Ted Williams*, Williams "worked on hitting five, six, seven hours a day, five, six, seven days a week, for seven years." It's probably worth pointing out that baseball gave Williams an escape from a tortuous family life—his father was largely absent and his mother was as obsessed with the Salvation Army and pounding the sidewalks of San Diego as Williams was about baseball.

Because American Legion and high school baseball were limited to older teens, adolescents who wanted to play in organized leagues were mostly out of luck until the late 1930s. That's when a twenty-eight-year-old Pure Oil Company clerk named Carl Stotz decided to make the world safe for youth baseball.

Stotz says he got the idea for Little League one day in August 1938. He was playing catch with his two young nephews in his backyard when the ball rolled away. As he chased it, his leg became entangled in a lilac bush. A New York Times orbituary for Stotz (he died in 1992) recorded what happened next:

> "As he frequently recalled it, Mr. Stotz banged a leg against the bush, then while he sat on the back steps and the pain subsided, he suddenly blurted out to his nephews: 'How would you like to play on a regular team with uniforms, your own cap, a new ball for every game and bats your size?'"

And so it was done. Stotz laid out his own field of dreams: sixty feet between bases (instead of ninety), forty-six feet from the pitcher's rubber to home plate (instead of sixty feet and six inches). On June 6, 1939, Little League took its first breath when Lundy Lumber administered a severe beatdown to Lycoming Dairy, 23-8.

"Little League defined the emotional geography of American suburbia," writes Charles Euchner in his 2006 book on the subject, *Little League, Big Dreams*. Men returning from the battlefields of Europe and Asia poured themselves into GI-Bill-financed educations, salesman jobs, newly created suburban tracts located near newly created shopping centers and, as a sign of middle-class propriety, youth baseball fields.

For the first time in American history, a generation of fathers was able to set aside free time to spend with their children. Instead of leaving work at the end of the day to retire to the local tavern or play in their own adult leagues, men volunteered in droves to coach their sons' baseball teams (girls would have to wait a few more decades). One can only wonder how many of those 1950s fathers needed time on the baseball field to heal their own lives as well, reclaim some childhood innocence they missed out on while growing up in an era of a global depression and world war.

In the 1950s, other youth baseball leagues popped up, each fiddling with the formula just a bit to set itself apart. PONY baseball, the association that my park belongs to, emerged in the summer of 1951 in Washington, Pennsylvania, and focused on thirteen- and fourteen-year-old players who were too old to play in Little League programs and not old enough for American Legion. PONY depicts a reared-up stallion in its logo but is actually an acronym that sounds like something J. Edgar Hoover might have sanctioned—"Protect Our Nation's Youth."

Also in 1951, the founders of the current Babe Ruth League met at the historic Yardville Hotel in Hamilton Township, New Jersey. A few years later, the association convinced the widow of Babe Ruth to lend the Bambino's name to their organization. These days, Babe Ruth also features the Cal Ripken Division, comprised of Major, Minor, Rookie, and T-Ball Divisions.

A year after Brown versus Board of Education guaranteed all citizens equal protection of the laws, Dixie Youth Baseball was established in 1955. This southern renegade association, which has long since cleaned up its act, got its start when South Carolina's sixty-one all-white Little Leagues resigned their charter rather than play in all-star tournaments with the state's only all-black league.

The recreational league concept of these associations now seems downright quaint in today's era of travel ball. In rec leagues, a reasonable attempt is made to balance teams with players of varying skills and experience, and to play games with a reasonable mix of good sportsmanship and skills development. Of course, there are always dads who will try to game the system, but what can you do? Baseball is a control freak's dream come true.

League play offers a certain comfort zone: you play against the same teams—the same children and parents—from your local zip code. Someone isn't likely to pull a nasty hidden ball trick on you, not when your families are sitting next to each other, or your business depends on word of mouth.

So it took youth baseball programs about fifteen years to go from teenagers to adolescents, then another fifty years to embrace everyone from five- and six-year-olds on up, including girls and disabled children. And in the last two decades, we've seen travel ball go viral with parents who want to refine their children's skills and to compete at ever-higher levels, perhaps increasing the chances of players getting into the college/professional baseball pipeline.

A 2006 *New York Times* article estimates that 30,000 teams are playing travel ball, as opposed to recreational league play. The greatest concentration of teams is in states like Florida, Texas and California, where the sun—and former players who offer private lessons and coaching services—abound.

In 2005, *The Dallas Morning News* looked into the amazing growth of tournament organizations and world series championships. The article reports that twenty-one organizations (ten new ones since 1993) conduct national or world series tournaments, with most holding championships in at least eight age groups, some dividing each age group into two or three classifications, others even hosting summer and winter championships. This means that more than two hundred and fifty teams could be crowned national or world series champions in a given year. That's a lot of world series rings available in child sizes. One local travel team reportedly played 300-plus games in five years and spent about $500,000 in out-of-state trips and vacations.

In metro Atlanta, the gold standard for travel ball is East Cobb baseball. Located outside the I-285 perimeter in the northern suburbs, this program is known throughout the U.S. as a mecca for top baseball talent. At one time, the Atlanta Braves featured three East Cobb alumni in their starting lineup—Jeff Francoeur, Brian McCann and Kyle Davies.

The top East Cobb teams practically guarantee Division-I scholarships for their starters. The coaches have college or professional experience, the facilities are minor-league quality, and scouts flock to their games. (According to a 2009 article in *The Atlanta Journal-Constitution*, East Cobb Baseball had a $1.1 million operating budget in 2007, with a revenue of $404,572 collected from tournaments and showcases.)

What's the downside? Besides the high cost that few families can afford (about $3,000 annually, not counting hotel and travel), there's the pressure.

Not just the intense pressure on children to become road warriors at a tender age, but the pressure on parents to figure out what's best for their children. Twenty years ago, the only option was the neighborhood baseball park before reaching high school. Now the options have proliferated like cable channels, and if you don't pay premium, you can't help but feel like you're being left behind.

This great schism between recreational leagues and travel teams is in the back of my mind when we find ourselves matched against an East Cobb travel team in one of our next games. The tournament is another warm-up for our guys as we head towards the all-important PONY district qualifiers in a few weeks. From the dad-coaches' perspective, we just want our guys to face some decent competition.

But the Bulls are seeing red. They've heard of East Cobb all their lives. A few of them have friends who play under the banner, and all of them wonder if they are good enough to play East Cobb baseball themselves. In the dugout before the game, they talk about how much they want to win. I'm just hoping they don't get crushed.

Today the Skipper has decided to start our little junkballer on the mound. He can be wildly inconsistent—even his father jokes about how his son's delivery changes from pitch to pitch. But when he's on, he can totally baffle hitters, especially the kind who have been trained to take a consistent, some would say machine-like, approach to hitting like most of these East Cobb players.

Before the game, the Skipper reviews hitting and running signs with the players. "You have to make yourself concentrate on a hot day," he says. The same could be said for our parents. After struggling to hang a plastic tarp over the bleachers, they finally give up. Meanwhile, in a matter of minutes, the moms and dads on the East Cobb team have erected a nice sturdy little pavilion that shades their little section of camp chairs.

In the bottom of the first inning, after we go down 1-2-3, I watch as the East Cobb first base coach, who looks like an ex-NFL football player, hikes up his shorts and goes into a slight crouch on the balls of his feet before each pitch. This is the kind of things that boys also notice. Unlike our collection of dad-coaches, he's the real deal—his clothes and shoes come from athletic wear catalogues. Our stained khaki shorts and worn-out cleats can't compare. He says things like "pull that bottom hand." I don't even know what that means, although that won't stop me from saying it at our next practice.

After two innings, East Cobb has a 2-1 lead. The good news, however, is that our pitcher is on today. His curveball is nasty. With his head, arms, legs and feet shifting, shuffling and darting in different directions each time he cuts the ball loose, the East Cobb boys can't find his release point. A few of them, after striking out and walking back to the dugout, shrug at the coaches and players with a "how am I supposed to hit that" expression.

When we come up to bat in the top of the third, we start the inning off with a bang—and a pratfall. The Bambino drives a pitch deep into the centerfield gap. But as he steams toward second base, he stumbles and falls to his knees about ten feet away from the bag. Our guys in the dugout are screaming with laughter as he tries to scramble to his feet, then finally gives up and begins crawling on his hands and knees towards second, arriving just before the throw. He stands up slowly with a tired grin. Everyone is laughing, boys on both teams, even the field ump; everyone it seems but the Skipper coaching third base.

The next batter gets an infield hit, moving the Bambino over to third. Then the Skipper calls for one of baseball's most daring maneuvers, a suicide squeeze. For the uninitiated, this play requires two things to happen simultaneously: the baserunner on third must bolt for home as soon as the pitcher starts his motion towards the plate, and the batter must lay down a bunt. If he misses, the runner is out cold.

To call a squeeze play with the Bambino on third, after his recent performance at second, takes a lot of guts.

When everything works like it's supposed to, it's a beautiful thing—and the coach looks like a genius for forcing a run in. But when it fails, it can be very demoralizing—and everyone blames the coach for trying to look like a genius.

This time it works. Like a dream. A beautiful bunt that rolls and stops a few inches away from the foul line as the Bambino chugs home. We tie the game, 2-2.

A few minutes later, while our first base coach talks on his cell phone with a customer, one of our guys hits a ground ball through the right side that the outfielder bobbles. We go up 3-2.

We're playing good, way over our heads. I wonder how long it'll last.

In the dugout, Henry walks by me carrying his catcher's mask and says quietly, "Now my other knee hurts."

I've lost track of him since we arrived this morning—I don't remember his first knee hurting. But he's taking the brunt of catching those nasty curve balls in the dirt, and he's already cut down one runner trying to steal. It's brutally hot. His face is flushed and flecked with clay and sweat.

"Get some water," I say, trying to keep my voice neutral.

"I'm just telling you."

I lower my voice, knowing that other players are watching and wondering how this will play out. "Don't tell me unless you want to come out of the game."

I don't like taking this tone with him, but as any dad-coach will tell you, you tend to treat your own flesh-and-blood a little tougher in the dugout than anyone else. One reason is that, frankly, you can. After measuring out patience and compassion in teaspoons to other players, sometimes you've got nothing left for your own.

A few minutes later Henry comes up to bat with two outs and the bases loaded. One good swing and we can really knock these guys back on their heels. The first pitch to him is a curve. In practice and before games, we drill it into these guys' heads that you never swing at curves until you've got two strikes. So it's more frustrating than usual to watch Henry hit an easy groundball to the shortstop. Inning over. As he walks back to the dugout to put on his catcher's gear, I make sure that I'm walking away so our eyes don't meet.

In the fourth inning, we still hold a 3-2 lead, and now we've got the attention of the East Cobb moms. They've left their shaded pavilion to sit in the front row of the bleachers near the fence, where they start chanting, "Gut check! Gut check!"

In our dugout, Coach Sam looks up from his scorebook and smiles. "Oh good, we've sent them into gut check."

For the next two innings, their groundballs hop right into our infielders' gloves, and twice they go three-up, three-down.

With only six more outs to go, I look up into the blue sky and watch as five crows fly slow and low, black wingtips almost touching each other.

What the hell does that mean?

I'm not usually superstitious, but now my primitive brain has taken over. These five crows can't be good. With the moms continuing to chant "Gut check!", we've entered the final minutes of some wrenching Greek tragedy.

And I'm wishing I didn't drink that extra cup of dark Colombian coffee while speeding to the ballpark this morning. It's hot, I'm dehydrated, hungry, and we're fighting for our lives on the plains of Tyrone, Georgia.

In the sixth inning, our pitcher continues to work his magic on the increasingly frustrated batters. Henry is working his butt off behind the plate. The East Cobb sluggers loft up three easy fly balls that our outfielders handle with ease. We're only three outs away from a victory for recreational leagues everywhere.

In between innnings, Coach Sam and I talk with the Skipper about bringing in a new pitcher, somebody who will just throw fastballs. But the Skipper wants to stay with our junkballer. Yes, he's thrown a lot of pitches, probably too many. But he's not walking anybody, and they simply cannot hit him.

This must be the kind of moment that gamblers live for: we're all in, everything is riding on the line, and in just a few minutes we'll know if we played the hand correctly or not.

After our batters go three up, three down, we take the field for the seventh inning. The first pitch is a ball. So is the second, third and fourth.

The first pitch to the next batter plunks him.

So that's what the five crows were telling me. After five pitches, East Cobb would get two batters on base with no hits, no outs. Next time I'll know.

Now we're in trouble. And the other team knows it. For a bunch of seasoned travel ball players, they act giddier than I would have expected. They are laughing and chattering and hanging on to the dugout fence. Their moms have dropped the "gut check" business and gone back to sit in the shade. I can feel the glorious endorphins and testosterone and whatever else draining away. My hope for a glorious win, the triumph of our little all star team, starts to sour.

We intentionally walk the next batter. The bases are loaded, so we need to get the out at home. We bring the infield in. We need one of those nice groundballs that bounces straight into our gloves. Please, God, please.

The batter hits a little blooper to leftfield. It should be an easy catch. But it's in that little Bermuda triangle of left field, centerfield and deep shortstop. The ball plops safely in the grass. Tied game, 3-3.

The next batter stands in. Bases loaded, no outs. Our tired pitcher reaches back and throws one more spinner towards Henry behind the plate. The ball bounces in the dirt in front of the batter and skips by Henry—he runs back to the fence, slides on his knees, throws the ball back to the pitcher who is covering the plate, but it's too late. Run scores. Game over.

I wish it didn't hurt so much, but it does. It hurts that we left our pitcher in too long, that our centerfielder didn't catch the blooper, and that Henry let the final curveball get by him. It hurts to see some of our players, including Henry, in tears after the game, and to see the tired, drained faces of the parents. It hurts that we didn't notch a symbolic victory for old-fashioned recreational-league summer teams that play together for weeks over high-stakes travel ball teams that collect frequent-flyer points.

Sometimes youth baseball just hurts like hell.

- 8 -

IN OUR SANDLOT GAMES, it was rare for the action to build into a nail biter. Usually, someone would bicycle home for a family dinner or get pissed off and leave, a real rally killer. Sometimes the drama would break into farce if the kid with the only ball decided to leave early—and the rest of us decided to over-rule his decision to take the ball with him. Sometimes the tree would eat the ball—and sometimes the ball would be brand new, the crisp white tissue and little cardboard box still lying on the grass.

Most of the time we quit because of darkness. I can only remember a few games that actually came down to the final out of the final inning—and those moments felt epic, as if everything we were doing would pass into legend and never be forgotten.

Baseball came into my life at the perfect moment. Maybe it does for everyone who takes the game seriously. In my case, baseball gave me a place where I could feel like a master of the universe. It gave me a reason to feel optimistic—I had a great future ahead—one day I would be a professional baseball player who lived on a ranch and drove a Corvette.

Unlike my sons, however, I didn't learn about the game firsthand from a coach in that sort of oral tradition that takes place in youth baseball. Over the years, watching this take place, I've seen my sons gain more confidence in themselves and in working with men outside their family, men who share their dugout, field and the emotions of winning or losing.

In my sandlot world, fathers went missing. They worked hard during the week and disappeared into chairs in front of the TV at night. Most of them knew how to make themselves scarce from the demands of wives and children on the weekend as well. The only time they came to the park where we played was to drag some poor offending soul home. Among my best friends, one father stayed home all day on disability leave (although we all knew he snuck off to go hunting in Wisconsin once a year); one father was divorced and never accounted for; and one was an alcoholic who disappeared from view for long stretches. My birth father was unknown, my adopted father was dead, and when my adopted mother remarried a little over a year later, my new stepfather, a stereo salesman at Montgomery Wards who would soon become a Life of Georgia insurance agent, brought stability to our home, even if he had no interest in baseball.

Fortunately, an adult came into my life around this time who spoke the language of sports, which

I understood then to be the secret language of manhood.

In his first sermon at Our Lady of Angels church, whose heavy front doors faced Interstate 10 on the worn-out fringes of downtown Jacksonville, Father O'Neil introduced himself by saying he was from Chicago, that he loved the White Sox and that, although he tried, he had little charity in his heart for the team on the other side of town.

Father O'Neil was in his 50s, stocky and tanned from spending long hours outside. He didn't look at all like the other priests assigned to our poor parish church, men who were tired and frail, and headed soon to the retirement home.

From my chair on the other side of the altar, I smiled knowingly along with the men in our congregation, mostly Syrians, Italians and Irish, from families who had landed in the port city of Jacksonville to work on the docks or railroad. The women acted as if they were flustered, but I believe most of them were simply titillated. I'm not sure any priest had ever mentioned baseball at the pulpit before, or any sport that didn't involve Notre Dame. And most attempts at humor were directed at the lack of air conditioning during the summer.

Mass became an interruption for me. Father O'Neil and I talked about baseball (football in the fall) while he dressed in his vestments before mass and while I moved around in my robes preparing the cruets of wine and water. As soon as mass was over, we picked up our conversation with hardly an interruption. Mostly he mused on his White Sox, saying with a little luck (here he would give a sign of cross) this might be their year. He would ask about my Orioles. My Orioles. No adult had ever talked to me like that before. And I was proud to talk about my Orioles. Since my parents had lived and met in Baltimore before the war, I felt that allowed me to adopt them as my team. It didn't hurt that they won the World Series in 1966 behind the awesome Robinsons—Brooks at third, Frank in the outfield—and were building one of the greatest pitching staffs of all time.

For the life of me, I couldn't understand why Father O'Neil simply didn't switch his allegiance from the losing Sox to the Orioles. In my opinion, his team would never be better than the Yankees and seemed destined to always fall short. At the time, I didn't realize that most people don't have a choice about who their team is—that it's usually part of your birth right, something determined by family ties and geography.

The facts about Father O'Neil's life were sketchy to me. He died before I was old enough to appreciate how much his kindness meant to me as a child. He must have grown up in the shadow of the 1919 Black Sox scandal. He once told me that before he became a priest, he wanted to be a ballplayer. Then he tried his hand at sports radio broadcasting before entering the seminary. Of all his assignments, his favorite church was one in Cuba where he coached a team of young men who had the softest hands he had ever seen. Years later I would understand that "soft hands" was a compliment to a ball player.

When he and I talked, he never preached to me. Instead he asked questions and listened, the only adult outside a classroom who ever did. He made me feel that my voice counted for something, that our love of baseball made us equals. My last experience with him came many years later when I was in high school and had fallen far away from the Church.

Out of the blue, Father O'Neil called my house and said he had two tickets to a Jacksonville Suns minor league game that evening. Would I like to go?

On the drive over, he asked if it would be okay if he removed his collar and if I would call him Jack at the game. He explained that he was only doing it so people around us could relax. He didn't want to ruin anyone's fun. I nodded as if this was a perfectly normal request.

At the game, we blended in perfectly. When a couple of guys behind us started ragging on the umpire, Jack nodded in agreement. I half-hoped that something would happen where he would suddenly have to reveal himself as a priest, perhaps to administer the last rites to a dying person in the stands. But the evening passed without drama.

A few years later I moved a few hundred miles west to attend Florida State University and never returned home to live or to visit the old church. Years after that, I heard from my mother that Father O'Neil retired and moved to "the old priest's home" near Villanova, outside of Philadelphia.

When I told the story of the Jacksonville Suns game to someone who who teaches a class at Emory about the history of baseball, he suggested that Father O'Neil may have had another reason for his ploy: that he had more in mind than making bleacher folks more comfortable at the game. That perhaps he was anticipating the special space where the game would be played. When "Father O'Neil" transformed himself into "Jack," he and I were no longer sharing the game as priest and parishioner (and ex-altar boy), but as equals who were alone together, but in a crowd.

When fathers take the field with their sons, they share a similar experience. They are alone together in a way that allows them to see each other in a new light.

- 9 -

"Whose team is *it anyway*?" my wife asks. Last night my fellow dad-coaches and I were, in Coach Sam's words, "overserved" at a neighborhood bar.

Now it's Thursday morning, and I'm hungover and trying to think of a reason why four grown men would talk about youth baseball for almost five hours nonstop.

In the next room, the PlayStation game goes quiet. Henry wants to hear my answer, too.

Whose team is it?

It's a good question. We start our long-awaited PONY district tournament next week. The remarkable patience that Alicia has shown towards my fling with twelve-year-old baseball is wearing thin. Not only did last night's outing use up my goodwill capital at home, but according to reports that trickle in later, at the homes of other dad-coaches as well. The Skipper says that the air conditioning in his house went out around 2 a.m.; that's when his wife noticed he wasn't home to fix it. Three of us saw opossums roaming around our yards and garages as we pulled into our driveways last night. Like the crows over the outfield, that can't be a good sign.

The baseball vortex has also swallowed up available time I might be spending with my older son. In a few weeks, Daniel is flying to Hanover with his German-born grandmother—it's the first time he'll be out of the country. In only two more years, he'll be away at college. Yet here I am spending almost all of my free time with the little brother. Sixteen-year-old boys are masters at hiding what they're feeling, but I can tell this is grating on him. When he asks why the water in our above-ground pool is the color of pea soup, he's only trying to remind me that there's more to running a family than his brother's baseball team. (I like Henry's attitude towards the pool better—he says now it's easier for his friends to hide underwater when they play Marco Polo.)

The pool is just one item on a growing list of things I'm neglecting until the season is over. One look at my front yard and peeling window trim would lead anyone to believe that the owner of the house has fallen on hard times.

Whose team is it?

Of course, Alicia wants to hear it's about the boys. And it is. Mostly. But I know what she's thinking because I'm thinking the same thing—when is the last time that we went out and talked all night? She's in graduate school this summer and would love nothing more than to share stories about the classroom and her fellow students. But, honestly, when she comes home from school and starts talking, I have a hard time following the ins and outs of library sciences. I find myself quickly losing track about alternatives to the Dewey Decimal system (who knew there were so many ways to organize books?), growing more impatient, itching to talk about what excites me these days.

Such as. . . what are we supposed to do about the pitcher who grooved two fat homerun pitches in his last two outings? Last year, he was practically unhittable. But since then he's added some extra pounds, and guys are catching up with his fastball. Do we spend more time on him because of his past success? Or do we invest time in someone else, like the new kid who keeps lobbying, along with his father, for more time on the mound?

And what to do with the outfielder who always drifts under fly balls and usually arrives a second too late. He's a funny kid who likes to joke about his attention deficit disorder. But it's not funny when he lets a ball drop that is perfectly catchable.

In the last game, after watching him put on the brakes to let a ball land safely in front of him, the

Skipper said quietly, "Does he know if he catches that, it's an out?"

And what to do about Henry's hitting? He's come down with the dreaded "stepping in the bucket," which is what hitters do when they're nervous about being hit by the ball. I've tried to stop worrying about it or feeling personally responsible for it. But sometimes when I see him relaxing at home, I think to myself that we should be outside exorcising the demons from his swing.

The team is my last thought at night and first in the morning. This must be what it feels like to be an addict. Work and other responsibilities seem negotiable as long as there's a game in sight. I wonder how many dad-coaches go off the deep end during the course of a season, jeopardizing jobs and relationships?

Whose team is it?

I'm bicycling down a downtown street with Henry and a few of his teammates. Suddenly, a reporter steps up beside me and asks if I've got a minute for an article he's writing about youth baseball. I tell him to go ask someone else. I'm busy.

It's yet another weird youth baseball dream.

Before one of our practices, Coach Sam shares one of his own. He's arriving at his office in the morning and is greeted by a group of Japanese architects. Then he remembers that he's supposed to be their corporate host for the day—and is totally unprepared.

In the last couple of weeks, the other dad-coaches and I have bonded in a way that is rare for men our age outside of work or the military. Years ago, I had friends who talked about their Robert-Bly-inspired experiences of retreating into the woods for three-day weekends of drums and poetry with other guys. "How peculiar and self indulgent," I thought at the time. Now people see me and my fellow dad-coaches talking about one thing and one thing only, The Team, and I know they must be thinking the same thing.

- 10 -

THE SKIPPER CALLS to say practice is on even though a few hours earlier a summer thunderstorm churned through the park and left behind a soggy mess. He says we can hit in the batting cages and then find some high ground for a little practice. Frankly, the news makes me feel a little grumpy. I was hoping for a night off.

When I tell Henry the news, he looks up from his PlayStation baseball game to see if I'm serious. "Is this about us trying to get tougher?" he says.

I nod. Obviously, he's heard the coaches talk in private because this has become one of the Skipper's favorite themes.

As we leave the house, I mention to Daniel that the last time it rained this hard, the entire outfield was flooded with several inches of water. Just enough to float a kayak.

He puts his guitar down and heads out the back door with us.

Daniel's twelve-year-old baseball experience was the opposite of Henry's. He dabbled in pick-up games and a little recreational city league before deciding he wanted to play in a more competitive league at Medlock Park, where we've been involved since. A neighbor heard of his interest and said he would pass along a recommendation to a friend of his, one of the coaches who would be drafting players. Later I asked him how he described Daniel to his new coach.

"I said he's a beginning player, but he's smart. And his family wouldn't give him any headaches."

At the first Medlock practice, I brought my glove to the practice, feeling sure that I would be asked to volunteer. Then I met Coach Tom and his assistant coach, who just happened to be two of the most knowledgeable baseball men in the park and fathers of two of the best players in their age group.

A few minutes after Daniel joined the team on the field, I took a seat in the bleachers and stashed my glove under my leg. Coach Tom ran his practices with the precision of a minor league instructor. I had no idea that hitting, catching and throwing could be broken down into such basic steps. Or that, without ever raising his voice, a coach could run such a disciplined practice.

Daniel was a neophyte who took his training seriously and everything else in stride. As a twelve-year-old rookie, even in this recreational league, he was starting much later than everyone else, something a few of the parents in the stand would mention every now and then after he struck out, which he almost always did. If it bothered him, he didn't show it.

It was humbling for me to see him fail so often, even joke about it, yet never give up. And fortunately he had a coach who helped him see himself as a work-in-progress, rather than as a failure whose strike outs were killing rallies.

By the end of the season, Daniel had managed to scrape out a few hits and walks, and turned into a decent right fielder who would dive for line drives in the gap. He became known as a smart player on the team and a pundit on the bench.

The games were surprisingly, shockingly, well-played and intense. On a clear spring night, the championship game ended 1-0, with two pitchers battling it out, and the other team on top. Afterwards, parents sipped beers in plastic cups, and boys ran around the infield playing pickle. Among the boys was seven-year-old Henry. The next season, he entered the Pinto draft. That's how, one step at a time, I was lulled into the cult of organized youth baseball.

For his part, Daniel stuck with the game long enough to make the JV baseball team in his freshman and sophomore years, where he enjoyed the view from the bench. When he decided not to try out for baseball during his junior year and instead to write about sports for the high school newspaper, it was the right call. He enjoyed interviewing coaches more than he did playing for them. In college, he became the editor of the student newspaper.

As we drive up to the batting cages at Medlock Park, the Skipper is sitting on top of a picnic table. He shakes his head slowly when he sees Daniel's red kayak on the roof of our van. "This isn't summer camp," he calls out.

Unfortunately, the creek hasn't spilled over its banks to flood the baseball field. So instead of cruising around the infield, Daniel launches himself down the muddy, swirling water of the creek and disappears around the bend. I can tell that Henry would love nothing more than to wait for his turn in the kayak, but he doesn't complain as we walk back to the van, grab the ball bags and ball bucket, and head to the batting cages.

One by one, the boys stumble out of cars in the parking lot. They seem surprised to see each other here. And since the other teams have stayed home this evening, they have the soggy, misty park all to themselves.

It's a little dreamlike: the very familiar park and the very unfamiliar sensation of being the only ones there. In fact, this will turn into one of those nights of baseball magic that many of them may remember for years to come. When they come back to this park as grown men, perhaps in the company of their sons and daughters, they may recall a few shards of games scattered throughout their six or so years of playing on these fields. But I'm guessing this night may stand out for many of them. (In the three years since these events took place, I've already heard players refer to this night as if it already was a worn-smooth legend.)

For the first hour, they do the usual batting practice at the cages, taking turns hitting balls thrown to them by one of the dad-coaches, or hitting off the tees on the side of the cages. Sometimes I think of these batting cage practices as feeding time at the zoo: we gorge them with balls thrown half-speed down the middle of the plate, and they react like big cats.

After everyone has taken a few turns in the cages and at the tees, we walk over to the largest field in the complex, the Pony field, where the thirteen and fourteen year olds play. The light mist is bright and sparkly above us where it meets the high outfield lights, gradually fading as it meets the wet grass. The smells of the creek on the other side of the fence, the wet earth and leather gloves, all blend together into one deeply satisfying pastoral smell.

I've heard other men refer to this field as the crown jewel of the park. It's impressive to look at—300 feet down the lines is a good poke—and seems even bigger because of the smaller fields in its immediate vicinity. But its grandness really comes from the fact that this is where most boys finish out their regulation baseball days.

This is where they run ninety feet to first base, where they see 80 mph fastballs released from man-sized hands, where they have their last chance to hit one out of the park. It's where they learn to appreciate the nuances of a squeeze play in a major-league playoff game. The parents who witness the games at this field are usually older and quieter and scarcer, making the action seem even more solemn.

Normally the big boys who own this field would be out here flexing their biceps, rubbing the stubble on their chins and intimidating our guys with every little grin. But tonight, it's just us, with one exception. The Skipper has invited Daniel's former coach, Tom, to lead the team in a few outfield drills.

How do you get to be the alpha dad-coach at a baseball complex? One way is by showing up at the ballpark—when you've already called off team practice—just to see how the fields looks, which is what Coach Tom is doing this evening.

He needs no introduction to the boys. It's enough that he's coached some of their older brothers and they've seen him holding court at the park for about half their lives. As he starts explaining the first drill to them in right field, talking to them as if they were high school varsity players, they stand at attention. Henry looks like he's ready to jump through a burning ring of fire.

Coach Tom wants the players to face him, one at a time, then he'll throw the ball behind them.

"Turn your head," he says, "and the rest of your body will follow. Don't lose sight of the ball. Run with your eyes on the ball."

There is a poetry to lines like this.

Most of our guys, too amped up, run under the ball, lose sight of it, and at the last minute try to make a desperate catch in the wet grass.

"Put two hands on it—catch it tall," he says.

Henry performs like a show dog. He nails it. I'm proud of him.

The next drill is more complicated and involves three parts. Coach Tom flips a ball to each boy as the player runs towards him. Then the boy tosses the ball back, and starts running away, cutting to the right as if going out for a pass, and Coach Tom hits him with the ball. After catching the ball, the boy throws it back one last time, then runs like hell to catch the equivalent of a Hail Mary pass over his shoulder.

I slip into the back of line with the boys. No one says anything. Each is in his own little world, focused tightly on his turn. Normally, this is the last thing I'd do, that is, intrude into their practice, hog their fun. But tonight seems different somehow. It's like I've been moved by the Holy Spirit or something. This is my version of being at a tent revival and marching down the center aisle. I'll do it once, and then never again, I promise.

When it's finally my turn, Coach Tom and I nod at each other, then he treats me like one of the players. I run towards him, catch the first ball, toss it back, then run back and cut to the right and catch the second ball, throw it back, then turn and race towards the outfield fence. Looking over my shoulder, trying hard to keep my head from becoming a bobble-head, I see the ball fly in a high arc through the brightly shimmering night air.

At this moment, I'm in that zone where nothing else matters but the ball. I remember this dog-like moment well from childhood. When everything around me was messy or weird or confusing, I could suddenly focus my entire consciousness on a ball and connect in such a way—with a hit or catch—that it would vibrate for a long time afterwards.

As the ball starts its descent, I now see that my timing is a bit off, the ball is farther away than I thought, and I will need to catch it lower, below my waist, instead of gliding in and catching it tall. My eyes stay locked on it as I begin to go down to my knees, sliding in the wet grass. At the moment of impact, the ball lands in the palm of my catcher's mitt, but as my head bobbles slightly, my eyes flicker for a brief instant and the ball fizzles out and drops on the wet ground. Bummer. I pick up the ball and toss it back to Coach Tom.

"Thanks for trying out for the team," says the Skipper. "Maybe next year."

This gets a little chuckle from the other dads. The boys are too busy waiting in line to notice.

A few minutes later, the Skipper calls the players together in a huddle and thanks them for their hard work, declaring practice over.

It's like a bell goes off in their heads. Unleashed, without a word, they start running in different directions across the outfield and diving headfirst into the mud-slick grass. Two, three and four boys run alongside each other like oversized geese and launch themselves airborne, landing with a wet splosh. They run and run until they are wet and heavy and covered with mud. By the time Daniel returns with his kayak and his adventures from the creek (lots of deadfall and flotsam, he says), the boys resemble giant creek hellbenders.

Not surprisingly, when it's time to drive home, the dads grumble half-heartedly about getting their cars dirty. In the parking lot, they scramble towels, blankets and floor mats to protect their upholstery. Only one dad seems happy about the prospect—it's his ex-wife's turn to drive their son home.

- 11 -

THE BIG DAY FINALLY ARRIVES. Every baseball we've caught, dropped, thrown, hit or waved at this summer, every family dinner we've missed, every ballpark hotdog we've eaten, every sip of beer at every late-night dad-coach bull session has been aimed at the PONY regional tournament that starts this evening. If we lose three straight games, we're done. If we win, we play in the state rounds the following week, and if we keep winning, we could go to the PONY World Series in Washington, Penn. That's a terrifying thought.

Henry is quiet this morning and stays away from the PlayStation for reasons known only to him. Instead, he joins me in the kitchen and helps me grill Bubba Burgers on the stove.

"Don't flip them until the blood shows through," I say, reading from the back of the box. We wait. The house is quiet except for the sizzling of ground beef.

Finally, I break the silence. "How many runners are you going to throw out today?"

"Two," he says, eyes fixed on the patties.

"How many hits are you going to get?"

"Two."

"How many belt-high fastballs are you going to watch go by?"

He rolls his eyes.

After lunch, I sit in front of the computer and try to concentrate on the words that sprawl across the screen in a document that I'm supposed to be editing. I keep rereading the same paragraph, but my brain is like an old outboard motor that just won't start. What does make sense are the e-mail messages from other dads and coaches, which I open as soon as they hit my inbox. Between us, we keep up a constant chatter, like a terrorist cell waiting to leap into the action — although, come to think of it, terrorists would be more disciplined.

My other job today is to keep an eye on the weather. According to my Internet browser, a big green glob is headed towards the ballpark. Thunderstorms are barreling straight down I-20 from Birmingham to Atlanta, and the tournament is taking place at a little complex that sits about fifteen miles west of Atlanta and just a few miles off I-20. So the likelihood of a rain-out is adding to my general unease.

Eventually, I give up the pretense of working. Long before it's time to leave the house, I put on the pony suit.

PONY tournament rules are much stricter than your typical pay-and-play travel-ball tournaments. For one thing, PONY tournaments are limited to those teams whose players have played a full season in a PONY-affiliated league. And among the many rules that teams must abide by, including the purchase of special PONY patches and baseballs, coaches are required to dress out in full team uniform, what we refer to as "the pony suit."

Prior to today, we've shown up at games to coach like a bunch of guys coming or going from a family picnic. But today we must slip into white polyester stretch baseball pants, tuck in our blue polyester jerseys, buckle them with a cheap stretch belt, and finish everything off with long blue socks and cleats.

As I check myself out in front of the full-length mirror, Henry appears behind me in his matching uniform. "Pretty slick," he says.

I'm official all the way down to the white sliding shorts under the pants. The Skipper hinted about the need for sliding shorts at one of the last practices, as if he suspected I might not know better and show up wearing plaid boxer shorts.

It feels a little odd at first, going outside, wearing the pony suit. Just when I forget I'm wearing it, someone reminds me. A guy standing in line at the convenience store says, "Hey, Coach." At the field, a dad congratulates me for doing my part for the team, as if wearing the pony suit is a community service project. A mom gives me a once-over that is hard to read—empathy, perhaps.

The Bulls players react like Henry. Now that the coaches are dressed out in the same uniform, it can only mean one thing. This is the real deal.

The sky looks ominous at the baseball field. Big fat dark rain clouds encircle us. We crowd around the little batting cage—basically just a big net thrown over some support poles—that's located a few feet outside the centerfield fence.

The first game of the day is winding down with only a few innings left. We have a few minutes before heading over to our dugout, which the Skipper reminds the boys they must do together as a team.

Next to me, a few of our players are talking about the Beatles.

"Are they still alive?" asks the centerfielder.

"Two of them are," says Coach Sam.

"Who was the best one?"

"John Lennon," says the shortstop, who is taking guitar lessons.

"Some people believe Paul McCartney was best," says Coach Sam, a decent guitar player himself.

As we hang out by the fence and talk, I flashback to talking about the Beatles when I was a kid, only we wanted to know who was the better band, the Beatles or the Monkees, and didn't have anyone older than us to advise.

As the minutes tick off before our game, I realize that instead of looking forward to the game, I'm starting to feel really stressed out. We've talked about preparing for this tournament all summer long, and it's suddenly here. What if our players have a bad day and get blown out? Twelve year olds are a moody lot: one minute they can be swooping down for the kill like an eagle, the next minute they can be lying in the grass like a wounded rabbit. I want their hard work to be rewarded.

And I just hope that my anxiety doesn't spread through the group like a virus.

Across the field, near the third base dugout, the team we're going to play tonight gathers. They have a couple of big boys. But, wait.... On closer inspection, one of the boys has a goatee and an earring. So he must be a young coach, possibly the son of one of the coaches. That leaves one big boy. He's about 6'2".

But not too smooth, according to the Skipper. "Watch how high he picks up his feet when he walks."

A few minutes later, without warning, the low, dark clouds unleash a torrent of rain. Everybody runs for cover. Within minutes, a thick red soup of clay flows across the infield, through the backstop fence, turning the sidewalk into a shallow creek.

After ten minutes of this, the tournament officials declare the game rescheduled for tomorrow.

"Good," says a coach from the other team, who looks like a professional baseball player in his pony suit. "Keeps me out of the dog house at work for another day."

Twenty hours later, we're back at the park, back in our pony suits, eyeing clouds that are skudding from west to east, but aren't nearly as dark as the day before. I don't feel nearly as tight as I did yesterday. One reason, I believe, is that I, too, stayed out of the dog house at work, outlasting two committee meetings without being exposed for the brain-addled youth baseball junkie I've become.

At one meeting I even got a chance to bring up my baseball obsession with child psychologist Marshall Duke. The tweens are a critical time, he says, when its important for children to find themselves as part of a group. At this age, they are looking for a "same-sex, best-best friend," where they can discover the great power of each other. And out of these relationships comes the confidence to deal with the opposite sex. As for organized youth baseball, it allows them to be around adults in a way they can tolerate, while also giving them a sense of the relevance of history.

Duke says this is the age when children have many identity questions and try to define themselves. "Who am I?" they ask. Answer: "I am a kid who plays baseball."

But I'm not sure this question is limited to our children. Here I am at middle age, still trying to define myself. "Who am I?" I ask. Answer: "I'm a father who has rediscovered the simple joys of being involved in my son's life and letting myself go a little ball crazy."

As the players from each team take the field, an announcer in the little metal deer stand behind the backstop calls out their names over a tinny little p.a. speaker. One by one, our players step out and face their moms and dads, brothers and sisters, and grandparents in the bleachers. The little pre-game ceremony looks and sounds hokey, but when I hear my name called out as a coach and I join the line-up in front of the first base line, my heart beats a little faster. It's surprising how these little formalities can sneak up on you. None of our travel tournament games started with any ceremony, and you don't realize what's missing until you are called to stand quietly in front of your friends and family. We lower our heads as someone at the microphone asks, in God's name, for the umps to call a good game, for the coaches to lead the boys, and for the parents not to lose tempers. There's no mention of what the players should do, but if everyone else behaves, they should be fine.

As the scratchy recording of the national anthem strains out, we turn to face the outfield fence and look around for a flag, which is on a little stick that someone poked into the top of the left field fence. The recording seals the solemnity of the moment. It puts each of us in his own private space before we become one again.

It's showtime.

Lefty starts on the hill today for the all-important first game. But we're going to be watching him carefully. When he dropped his ball bag near the batting cage earlier, he was grimacing and slumping more than usual. The Skipper asked him what was wrong. He replied by opening his mouth to reveal a set of shiny new braces.

"You're not on any painkillers, are you?"

He shook his head slowly.

As we watched him slump miserably against the batting cage, the Skipper said to the coaches, "New team rule. No getting braces before pitching in the first game of an official tournament."

Fortunately, Lefty forgets all about the wires in his mouth once the game starts. After three innings, he's zooming right along, no hits or runs. But the ace on the other team is just as unhittable. The umpire is helping both boys by calling a huge, lazy strike zone, so lots of boys on both sides are looking at strike three on pitches so far off the plate that they probably couldn't reach them if they tried.

Before our boys go up to bat in the fourth inning, the Skipper pulls them together outside the first-base dugout for a little pep talk.

"Are you over your jitters yet?"

Most of the guys grin and nod. A few aren't quite so sure.

"Now go out and score five runs."

Our first batter lays down a perfect bunt, scampers to first base, where the pitcher fires the ball before realizing that neither the first or second baseman is covering. A few minutes later, one run is in and the bases are loaded for the Bambino, who drives a belt-high fastball over the left field fence, scattering the coaches from the first game who have gathered to scout our game.

As the bopper puts the finishing touches on his homerun trot and heads back into the dugout, I see his mother standing just beyond the gate leading to the dugout, hoping to catch his eye. I give her a thumbs up.

"I love it when he does that," she says.

Henry adds a double to the hit calvacade. Afterwards I watch him walk by me in the confined space of the dugout with a swagger that I haven't seen before. All the boys are strutting. The little dugout is their private clubhouse, and each one of them is a VIP.

If the grizzled old umpire is deliberately calling a huge strike zone to get the game in before the next round of storms arrive, he's wildly successful. We win in five innings after going ahead by ten runs.

In right field for the post-game speech, the boys take a knee. "You didn't play your best game," the Skipper tells them.

They look surprised.

"I can think of about ten misplays or missed signs. But now we're going to put that stuff behind us. Tomorrow night we play for the district championship. Any questions?"

The Bambino raises his hand. "Can we eat pizza after we win tomorrow's game?"

The players stop grinning when they see the serious expression on the Skipper's face. "We're playing a good team tomorrow—a team that is better than us at some things."

- 12 -

I VIVIDLY REMEMBER my first sandlot baseball game, but I have no memory of the last. After I was able to bicycle to other neighborhoods where school friends lived, see the world through their eyes and make other connections, the sandlot magic faded. By age thirteen, my sandlot days were over. I began riding by the park without seeing the diamond.

After 1969, my passion for professional sports crashed and burned. Both of my favorite teams suffered upsets that still go down in the history books as two of the all-time worsts. In Super Bowl III, the underdog New York Jets, led by Broadway Joe Namath, beat my Baltimore Colts. Then, in the fall of 1969, my Orioles, widely considered to have one of the best teams of all time, lost the World Series in five games to the Miracle Mets. More than most fans, I needed my teams to boost my self-esteem, not throw me under the bus then back up over me a couple of times.

In my teenage years I became indifferent about sports and religion (and politics). In college, I became a bit more cynical. It wasn't until 1991, after the birth of my two sons that I rediscovered the magic. This was also the year of the Miracle Braves, who made believers out of many of us.

- 13 -

On Wednesday afternoon, a few hours before it's time to put on the pony suit for the second game of the district tournament, I get an e-mail that says tonight's game has been called off because of rain. The fields are unplayable from last night's storms, and more bad weather is expected.

When I break the news to Henry, he launches into a little happy dance in the middle of the living room that ends with him diving onto the couch, then lying back and talking about what's on his mind.

"I think a little break is good, but I hope the game isn't rained out on Friday because I don't want to get into a slump," he says. "I think the reason why I got some good hits last weekend is because I'm not afraid anymore. I'm not stepping out. I know I can hit anybody."

"That's true," I say. "I haven't seen you afraid up there in a long time."

"I just wish I could move up in the batting order. But now the guys in front of me are all hitting good."

"That'll take care of itself. You just keep hitting the ball."

While Henry chats away, I realize I've got my own problems—a nasty scheduling conflict. Tomorrow night I'm supposed to be in the classroom teaching about fifteen adult students the basics of screenwriting. For the last month, I've skipped baseball practices to teach the four-hour weekly class at a local college. But tomorrow night could be the deciding game in the district championship game.

While trying to decide my next move, I recall an experience that happened about fifteen years ago. I was a grad student at the time in a journalism class at Georgia State University. The professor assigned us to write a feature article about a youth baseball game. He even gave us the day, time and location of the game, saying he would be there as well.

My classmates and I showed up, and we roamed the crowd, working diligently, everyone looking for his own particular angle. It wasn't until the second or third inning, when I heard the p.a. announcer introduce a player who had the same last name as the professor, that I realized what was going on. The class assignment was a cover so that he could watch his kid play. When the word spread among my classmates, we threatened to mutiny.

Only now do I understand what the professor was going through. Poor guy had it bad.

The next morning, the day of the game, I wake up from yet another weird dream. The Skipper and boys show up at my house wearing ties—in fact, each boy wears two ties—like a parody of college players who parade through the airport in jackets and ties. Suddenly the scene cuts to our guys watching a Braves game at Turner Field. At first I'm sitting with Skipper and boys. Then I wander off. The dream ends with me standing outside the stadium, not knowing how to get back inside.

During the day I go back and forth from responsible instructor self to my addled baseball junkie self. Finally, I make a call that, I admit it, puts me on shaky ground. My class is four hours long and usually I fill it with in-class exercises, short films and discussions.

But this Thursday, my students and I will meet for the first hour. Then they will have three hours to work on their screenplays in the lab. When I announce this in class, without breathing a word about the baseball game, they are understandably quite pleased. Some of them actually need to use the computer lab, but they're in the minority.

I try to act like everything's normal while I stand in front of the class going over their project, answering last-minute questions, but my heart is pumping like crazy from a combination of guilt and pre-game anticipation.

It's definitely a low point for me. For the past couple of weeks I've been feeling absentminded and neglectful at work. And now this. I try to justify it, saying that other instructors allow lab time, but the point is, I wouldn't be doing it if not for the district playoff game.

Outside a light drizzle is falling as I dash to my car in the parking lot. Traffic is inching along to the interstate entrance ramp, a few blocks away. My head is buzzing with AM-radio static. Cars are inching forward, the windshield wipers sweep back and forth, and I'm about twenty miles northwest from where I need to be.

I call Alicia for an update. Because of graduate school, she hasn't attended many games lately, but she made a point of attending this possible tournament clincher. She says the game before ours is still in the sixth inning. And it's not raining there.

"Are you still coming?" she says.

That she would even ask this makes me realize how little she knows what I'm going through.

Ten long minutes later I see the long line of cars ahead of me snaking around the entrance ramp trying to merge onto I-85. For all I know, the interstate could be blocked for hours. People who live in other parts of the country fear earthquakes, blizzards and floods. In Atlanta we fear traffic bottlenecks caused by overturned semi trucks that block all lanes for six hours.

I coast by some crepe myrtles trees in full red and purple bloom that are as soggy and shaggy as wet poodles. I crawl through the wide concrete corridor of the downtown connector, about ten lanes of traffic filled with thousands of poor souls like me. I'm hitting five miles per hour as I pass by a billboard that says the Braves game starts at 7:35. It's 7:34 on my dashboard clock. Normally I would listen to the pre-game show. But I can't today. I don't want to hear Skip and Pete talk about anything related to baseball that doesn't involve my son's game.

Up ahead, the traffic thins out. Two left lanes open up. I hit the accelerator, headed west, and finally ease up when the needle points to ninety. Thanks to youth baseball, I've turned into one of those scary Atlanta drivers who terrorize decent people on the highway.

From the parking lot of the baseball complex, I can see the visitor's dugout. To my surprise, the other team's coaches are standing around, waiting. The game hasn't started. Some how, some way, I made it.

I change into my uniform in the backseat of the car. Before I take off my pants and slip into my pony pants, however, I make sure no families are walking by. The last thing I need is to be arrested for indecent exposure. I walk away from the car without my cap. When I run back to get it, I almost get hit by a slow-moving car.

This is how people arrive at a game all worked up. It's not just another youth baseball game today. I skipped out of work. I risked life and limb to get here. It's a big deal. It's huge. It's Christmas, New Year's Eve, and the Fourth of July rolled into one.

I try to act nonchalant as I approach the dugout and nod to the boys waiting inside. Some ask me where I've been. Henry passes by me without saying a word. He has his game face on.

Coach Sam explains what's up. It seems that some unidentified person called the state coordinator of the PONY baseball association and told them we have two illegal players on our team. That is, illegal in the sense that they didn't play on a spring recreational team and don't qualify to be on this PONY tournament team.

Our coaches and parents wonder who would've made such a false accusation. Someone from the other team? An ex-wife? Frankly, I'm surprised that no one suspects me. After all, the game was delayed just long enough for me to make it.

After another five or so minutes, with the Skipper conferring with the coordinator on his phone, we are cleared to play as long as we can produce scorebooks in the next couple of days backing up our claims. (We do. Later it turns out that a father on the other team suspected that our lefty was a travel-team ringer.)

In the first inning of the championship game, our boys continue their hitting spree. Our leadoff batter gets a walk, then steals. Our second batter gets a hit. Our third batter drives one to the fence to bring in the first run. Our next guy hits a ground ball to make it 2-0. Our big bopper rattles the fence with a line drive. 3-0. So does the next batter. Henry hits a hard groundball, but it's straight at someone for the first out.

Their guys go three up, three down, against our lefty.

By the fifth inning, we're ahead 6-0. It's cruise control time when, just as quickly, the momentum shifts to the other team. With the help of a few close calls by the umpires (feeding our paranoia that home cooking is involved), the other team loads the bases with no outs. Then they score two runs with an outfield blooper.

On a count of three balls and two strikes, we bring our reliever in from shortstop. He's tight, and he hasn't warmed up.

His mom calls out, "You're okay, you're fine."

He's anything but fine, and he knows it.

They draw the game into a tie at 6-6.

When Henry tries to nail their runner stealing third, the ball skips by our third baseman. We're springing leaks. They go up 7-6.

Then Henry throws out the next runner trying to steal second base.

Three outs. Finally.

Over the next two innings, our boys bounce back, scoring four runs, with a homerun by the bopper to make it 10-7. Emotions start to boil over. The umpire calls time out to yell into our dugout to close the gate, which has been cracked open for the entire game.

Next he threatens to eject the Skipper for sneaking a cigarette behind the dugout between innings, which the Skipper has done every inning of every game this summer. When their infielders warm up, the shortstop overthrows first base by about ten feet, hitting the fence exactly where, on the other side, Coach Sam and I are talking.

After their pitcher hits the Skipper's son with a fastball, one of their coaches says to the Skipper at third base, "How'd you like that one, Coach?"

Baseball is all about avoiding emotion. That's why it's such a shock when it rises to this level among adults. But while much has been written about this being the dark side of youth sports, I also see it as the unavoidable human side. We can't get rid of primitive emotions in these games. Adults will say and do stupid things from time to time. This is part of the learning process—for children and adults—that we signed up for when we joined the team.

Before the old umpire declares the game over, our opponents push another run across, but we add a few more to make it 12-8. Thunder sounds in the distance as we get the final out and win the game to become PONY district champions.

The Skipper gathers the boys together in right field. He talks about how far the team has come in six weeks.

"Tonight, many teams would have folded up their tents and gone home after they fell behind. It doesn't get any tougher. We came out of the box fast, scored a lot of runs, then went on cruise control. Then stuff happened. That's when many guys would've folded."

He says the team fought back as hard as any team he's ever seen. He congratulates the pitchers on the fine job they did.

He asks if the coaches have anything to add.

I do. I want to congratulate a certain player.

"Before the game he said he was going to throw out two runners, and he did. Especially when we needed a big out. Nice job, Henry."

I did it. I've broken another baseball taboo. I praised my own son. But the spirit moved me. And as I look down at the hot, sweaty faces of the boys, none of them seems as surprised by my words as Henry.

- 14 -

THERE COMES A TIME in the lifespan of a youth sports team when most families have had enough. Enough leaving work early to drive in rush-hour traffic to reach hard-scrabble ballparks where your child may or may not play long enough to work up a good sweat. Enough fast food and not enough nourishing family dinners. Enough neglect of non-playing siblings. Enough looking at the calendar and wondering when do you get a real vacation. And yet, there are more games to play and it is, above all else, a team game.

Even as an obsessed dad-coach, I'm not immune to wondering "When do I get my life back?" But it's easier for me because I have no choice but to remain loyal to the team until the end, even if we should, God forbid, somehow keep winning games for the next six weeks and end up in the Pennsylvania countryside playing for the PONY World Series title.

In the parking lot, it's a different story. The other day I overheard two moms talking about vacations that start "when THIS is over with," as if they were talking about a skin rash. Several dads have voiced their concerns in public and private. "Geez, I know we want to win, but let's give some other kids a chance," said one normally stoic dad, a former college baseball player, who was gung-ho in the beginning about his son making the team, even if it meant sitting on the bench. Another dad, who I learned only recently works as a mall Santa Claus, is already making plans to have his son play in his former park next season. "We miss it. There was less focus on winning there. He had more fun."

You know it's rough when Santa lines up against you.

Yet another dad takes me off to the side and asks what his son needs to do to get more playing time. He says he doesn't understand it—his son works harder than anyone else out there. How can I tell him that despite his son's devoted work ethic and regular attendance at clinics and private coaching sessions, he still ranks below other players, especially with the game on the line? All I can really do is shrug and suggest he talk with the Skipper. And when the Skipper describes his private conversation with this dad and a few others, I nod and keep quiet.

I go back and forth on this issue of fair playing time. During our spring recreational seasons, Coach Sam and I follow this credo to a fault, even if it means pitching four boys against teams that trot out the same two aces for every game of the season. My older son, Daniel, rode the pine for two years on his high school JV team. He never griped—that was my job. I wanted to see him develop and grow, while the coaches played their favorites. How could a father not think otherwise?

Now, as we approach the big state tournament, I'm plagued by dark thoughts. I think how tempting it would be to play only to win. Unlike Little League, there's no rule that says we have to play everyone. This is cold, hard PONY baseball, which prides itself on being like the real thing. In the short run, things would be far easier if we just stuck with our top players to get the job done. We're not trying to be the Boy Scouts, where everybody has a chance to earn merit badges, right?

But I see long-term problems with this win-at-all costs mentality and, fortunately, so does the Skipper. The players and parents on our team are friends and neighbors, starters and benchwarmers alike. We see each other at school and the grocery store. As much as we all want to win, we agree that some things are more important, like substituting a player at second base in the middle of the game not for defensive reasons but because it's the fair thing to do.

Of course, this rubs a few of our parents the wrong way. They accuse the inner circle of trying to make everybody happy, as one dad of a regular starter says, "of giving in to the mommies." So we get it from both sides, and it falls to the Skipper to lead us through the wilderness of youth competition where the winner isn't always the team with the most wins, but the one where its players and parents are still talking to each other at the end of the season.

- 15 -

Finally, a baseball park with class. The PONY state tournament is being held at a beautifully renovated baseball complex in Buckhead, where million-dollar homes lie under old canopies of white oaks and hickories. The park was once a Muscogee Creek Indian settlement, then a Civil War battleground and eventually was transformed into a public park in the 1930s before sprouting ball fields in the 1960s that have received a complete makeover in recent years. With its pedestrian-friendly walkways and grandstands, manicured fields and warm-up areas, press box with professional sound systems, the complex makes the game feel special, the way it's supposed to be.

As we walk down the sidewalk to the batting cages, there's even a Hollywood quality to the slanting late afternoon sunlight. The boys look downright golden and heroic in this light as they step lightly in their cleats and fight back grins at how ridiculously cool this whole thing is.

Of course, we may be totally overmatched here. When it's time to introduce the players on the field, the players on the other team emerge from their dugout and hand out high-fives as if they've been doing it all their lives. One of their coaches barks "get some attitude" to a player who doesn't look chirpy enough. Our guys, meanwhile, perhaps in an effort to appear cool and understated, walk out and stand next to each other like suspects in a police lineup.

But the real answer comes in the first inning. One of their guys hits a rocket shot that is hooking into the left field corner. For some reason, our normally hesitant outfielder takes off on contact and makes a spectacular diving catch as the ball is about ankle-high off the ground. He then rolls over and flashes his glove—and the ball—to the umpire before jogging casually back to the dugout. Only his coaches and teammates and families know that this is the most unbelievable catch he's ever made.

A few innings later, in the dugout, he confides that he woke up this morning, watched SportsCenter on ESPN and saw a diving outfield catch just like his. He remembers fantasizing about doing the same. Our second baseman knows the feeling. After making a quick pivot to turn a sweet double play, a few minutes later in the dugout he said that it felt like something out of a dream. Immediately after doing it, he had the feeling that he had already done it before, exactly the same way.

Yes, we are playing over our heads today. Somehow, SportsCenter and our own dreams are shaping our reality. This leads me to wonder if, before games, instead of the usual infield practice, we should sit in the dugout and have the players close their eyes while we work on visualization drills.

We coast through the rest of the game and win easily. The highlight comes when one of our guys who has been riding the bench most of this short season drives a ball over the centerfield fence. He's running full-speed towards second base when he suddenly realizes what just happened. Then he raises his fist in the air and keeps sprinting until he crosses home plate. It's his first long ball ever and it may be the fastest homerun jog in history. Minutes later, we see his dad walking around the outfield fence to claim his trophy ball.

The next morning I can't work. I'm still buzzed from last night's win, and we have another game tonight. Being around a bunch of happy, victorious twelve-year-olds is a powerful rush—maybe I've got a contact high from their hormones. I could get fired from my job today, lose the mortgage on my house, learn that all my pets have been rounded up by animal experimenters, and I'd probably shrug it off because of our first win in the state playoffs.

Meanwhile, Henry spends the morning watching some of our old home movies and calls me in to join him. In a 1994 video, he's a long-haired two-year-old wearing a plastic knight jousting helmet, only the helmet is flipped around so it resembles a catcher's helmet. That was the year he watched the 1991 World Series videotape, Braves versus Twins, about a hundred times. One of his favorite games at that age was to pretend that the Braves had just won the playoffs, and he was Greg Olsen ripping off his catcher's mask to jump in my arms.

Later he comes across a video of his batting practice from three years ago. He calls me back into the living room. Sitting cross-legged on the couch, he says he can't believe how awful his swing was. Before each pitch, he helplessly lifts up his front leg and begins swiveling it toward third, as if to run away.

I remember those days well. He started stepping into the bucket not long after his cousin was hit in the face with a fastball, a horror that was relived over and over again in family stories. Henry's fears climaxed in a game that pitted his nine-year-old team against a travel team of gangly eleven-year-olds. The opposing pitcher looked like Ichabod Crane. The kid was throwing fastballs in the 80 mph range without any control whatsoever. Our players were ducking and hitting the dirt during each at-bat. When it was time for Henry to bat, he flat-out refused. It may be purely a coincidence, but two boys on that team never played baseball again after that summer.

Another beautiful evening. The sky is so clear that you can make out the feathery edges of clouds, a rare event in smoggy Atlanta. As we go through our warm-ups, the other team sits on the bench and studies us. "Just like real ballplayers," says Coach Sam. Usually, our guys spend this time roaming aimlessly around the dugout, looking for sunflower seeds or gum or talking about video games or TV commercials.

Before the game, the Skipper says he heard that baseball scouts are already keeping their eye on the 12-year-old pitcher we're about to face tonight. When the boy walks towards the batting cage, he has that loose, rolling gait of a seasoned athlete — someone who's grown accustomed to being the best player on the field and being watched.

We have reasons to be optimistic. We've got our tall lefty on the mound, and tonight he's pounding the zone. Their stud pitcher throws hard, but he hasn't settled down and is giving up a few walks, passed balls and little dingers. We go up 3-0 after two innings.

In the next inning, one of their guys delivers a hard line drive up the middle and makes it 3-2. A few pitches later, a foul ball comes straight back and knocks Henry to the ground. He gets to his feet slowly, the breath knocked out of him. The umpire calls time. The Skipper goes out to talk to him.

It's one of those moments where you watch your son from a distance and wonder how he's going to deal with a hard knock. As the Skipper and the umpire stand beside him on the field, Henry stands still, looking at the ground. Then he wipes his face with the sleeve of his jersey, puts his catcher's helmet back on and goes back to the plate. The fans in the bleachers, fans from both teams, clap for him. Later, when he returns to the dugout, he tells me that he popped a blood vessel—again—in his finger. I'm too proud of him to do anything but pat him on the back and say "hang in there." It also occurs to me that he may have a future in pediatric sports medicine.

We're down by two runs in the next-to-last inning, 6-4, when some of our fans enter the Ugly Zone for the first time this summer. It starts out simple enough. The Skipper protests a bad call that goes against us. He's frustrated and lets the umpires knows it. In retrospect, maybe he protests too much. There's a thin line between raising a ruckus because you're standing up for your players and showing up umpires. When the Skipper is done, one thing is clear: we won't be getting any favors from the men in blue.

Our parents are feeling the frustration as well. When one of our nonstarter outfielders lets a ground ball roll by him, not the first one of the game, one of our dads calls out loudly, "How can you miss it?" It leaves a bad taste in the air.

A few minutes later, the umpire calls out one of our players at second who, even to my untrained eye, is perfectly safe by a full step. This blatant injustice is the final straw for several of our fans. They start yelling and rattling the chain link fence in front of the bleachers, calling the umpires names and accusing them of throwing the game. Our players in the dugout watch this outburst in disbelief and even with a little bemusement.

We play on, but the negative cloud hangs over us for the rest of the game. Just when the game seems out of reach—we're down by two runs with two outs in the final inning—we put together a little rally and get runners on second and third with our number-three hitter up to bat. All we need is a base hit to tie the game.

He scorches the ball into the gap between second and third. You can't hit it any harder or seemingly in a better place. But just as suddenly as hope explodes in our hearts, the shortstop dives into the void and snags the ball out of the air. Ball game.

Heat lightning flashes in the distance as the Skipper gathers the boys together in shallow left field. "We could complain," the Skipper tells them, "but it won't make it any better. We've got to learn an important lesson here. Play through the bad calls. Keep your dignity. Keep your heads up. You played hard. Be proud of the way you played."

Tonight, instead of going off with the other coaches for our usual round of decompression and beers, I head home with Henry. As we inch out of the parking lot behind a line of other cars, Henry and I are quiet as Alicia describes her day at school and wonders how our son Daniel is doing in Germany. Maybe she's oblivious to our pain, or maybe she's trying to distract us. But I finally ask if we can just drive home in silence. Henry asks for a foot rub.

"Baseball is a worrying thing," I once heard someone say on the radio. Now we're down to the loser's bracket. We need to win three straight games to clench the state championship. The only bright side to this is that we don't have a game on Thursday, which means I won't be tempted to sneak out of another screenwriting class.

- 16 -

Friday evening. We've just finished the fourth inning and have bounced back from being down 4-0 to tie the game. Henry drove in the last two runs. When he walks back to the dugout, his teammates excitedly pound him on the back. Slowly he works his way over to me and says, "Now both of my knees hurt."

When we make out three, and as he puts on his catcher's gear, I jog out behind home plate to warm up the pitcher. While I've done this off and on before, always a little too eager, this time it's different.

Crouching behind the plate, seeing the well-groomed field under the bright lights as our guys warm up at their positions, I suddenly get it. The whole thing. The game's beautiful symmetry. The familiar, easy rhythms. Within the confines of that space, wild and unpredictable things might happen, but usually it's a place where one can just feel at home.

And what a view from behind home plate. The ball, first a pinprick of white, tumbles through the air, red laces spinning, smacking into the leather glove. So this is what Henry's world is like. It's so different from my dad-coach world of watching from the distance and stressing about this or that—and so different from my messy sandlot world where, dreamy as it could be, was always breaking down. The ball would sink into the upper branches of the palm tree and be lost forever, or big brothers would suddenly decide to pound smaller brothers into submission. Whenever I had moments where everything seemed to flow together, it was always about me, about what I happened to be doing, never about teammates pulling together or collaborating with adults.

Actually, until this moment it has never occurred to me how peaceful it is being inside the diamond. Do all the boys feel this way, or a degree of this, even if they can't talk about it? I hope so. What a revelation. As a child, I would've loved to have been part of this world.

We're leading 8-5 when the home team goes up to bat in the final half of the last inning. Our centerfielder misplays a ball and they score a run. Then a ball stays fair down the third base line and they put runners on first and third with no outs. The winning run stands at the plate.

We feel the game trickling away from us. My stomach is churning. So this is how it's going to end.

Sure enough, their big slugger gets his pitch and drives it into deep left field. The ball is sailing and hooking away from our outfielder, who is running at a full gallop and at the last possible moment, backhands and spears the ball.

Two outs later, the game is ours.

Now our team of sweaty, flushed, clay-streaked boys and dad-coaches gather in shallow left field. As usual, everyone waits for the Skipper to have the first and last word. This time he looks around and grins at all the boys, then takes a deep breath and says, "That was a lot of fun."

The boys aren't sure how to take this. The Skipper isn't known for using sarcasm in team huddles. Some of them smile in agreement; others exchange skeptical looks. Only the shortstop has the gumption to raise his voice and ask: "Where were you?"

- 17 -

THE SATURDAY AFTERNOON GAME marked the last running of the Bulls. It was the hottest, stinkiest day of summer. Not a cloud or breeze stirred. You could feel the steam rising from the earth as the sun slowly roasted it—and us. It was the kind of summer day that makes everyone question the sanity of playing baseball, especially with swimming pools close by. It was also a day that the dad-coaches would regret staying up late the night before during the backporch strategy session.

Henry got the rock and climbed the hill for the Bulls. He finished the game on the red-clay mound, fighting all the way.

What happened? The little things didn't go our way. Sometimes it goes like that. And so the season ended as quietly as it began. It ended with a feeling of hope dancing in our stomachs until the last possible moment, with our winning run on base, but the ball landing with a soft poof into the pitcher's glove instead of slipping by for a hit.

It ends in shallow left field with the Skipper addressing the boys, who are still wearing the infield dirt on their sweaty faces and jerseys. "We're proud of you," he says. "You gave everything you could."

It ends with the boys putting their hands together in the middle for one last time.

One. Two. Three. Bulls!

Weeks later. Our days are calmer. We spend less time in traffic and more time relaxing at home. I'm catching up with work, grateful to be able to concentrate for hours at a time on issues that have nothing to do with twelve-year-old baseball players.

You can look through the water of our little swimming pool and almost see the bottom.

One day, Henry walks behind my desk while I'm working at the computer and folds himself into my lap. "I miss playing baseball," he says.

The fall season is only a few weeks away.

Epilogue

After their twelve-year-old summer, the Bulls regrouped over two more summers, winning the state tournament as thirteen year olds and, as fourteen year olds, advancing to a district tournament held in Texas. Henry became a starting pitcher for his high school baseball team, the Chamblee Bulldogs, and is now playing baseball at LaGrange College, a Division III college about an hour's drive south of Atlanta. Every now and then I joke with friends about adopting a nine-year-old shortstop. They don't seem to realize that I may be serious.

Notes

For the section on the historical overview of youth baseball, I relied on the following sources:

Little League Online. History of Little League. Retrieved from http://www.littleleague.org/Learn_More/About_Our_Organization/historyandmission.htm

Steven Gelber, "Working at Playing: the Culture of the Workplace and the Rise of Baseball," *Journal of Social History*, Summer 2001.

Leigh Montville, *The Big Bam*, Doubleday, 2006.

Ed Linn, *Hitter: The Life and Turmoils of Ted Williams*, Harcourt Brace, 1993.

Charles Euchner, *Little League, Big Dreams: Summer Miracles, Kid Heroes and the Best World Series Ever*, Sourcebooks, 2006.

For anyone interested in reading more about the father-son connection in baseball, you'll find a handful of books still available. Perhaps the most literary — and the one with the best title — is poet Donald Hall's *Fathers Playing Catch with Sons: Essays on Sport*

(1984). Notwithstanding the title, Hall focuses mostly on the world of professional sports, not father-son relationships.

One of the best known Little League dad-coach accounts is CBS News correspondent Bill Geist's bestselling *Little League Confidential: One Coach's Completely Unauthorized Tale of Survival* (1995). Geist details the ups-and-downs of a season of Little League (Ridgewood, N.J.), basing it on nine years of coaching experience. He writes more from the perspective of a coach than a father, rarely zooming in on his pre-adolescent son or the emotions between father and son.

In *Joy in Mudville: A Little League Memoir* (2000), former Crawdaddy editor and political writer Greg Mitchell chronicles a season of Little League in Nyack, New York, providing rich play-by-plays of games and the emotions behind them. At times he reveals details about his relationship with his ten-year-old son, but mostly he looks at the wider context of youth sports with interviews featuring professional players and celebrities (circa mid-1990s).

In *The Way Home* (2001), literary agent Henry Dunow writes about coaching his seven-year-old son's team on Manhattan's Upper West side. He reflects on his experiences growing up in a postwar Jewish household with a literary father who had little patience with baseball. Dunow writes a literary account that alternates chapters about coaching with chapters about his coming-of-age.

Most recently, Boston Globe columnist Dan Shaughnessy in *Senior Year* (2007) looks at his son's senior year of high school. Shaughnessy's book is mostly aimed at parents who are focused on older players and the pressures of college recruiting.

I should acknowledge here how much I gained from sitting in on two classes at Emory University taught by Profs. Dana White and Peter Dowell on baseball and culture. Over the years, they have shared their knowledge and passion of the game with hundreds of undergraduates, which reminds me that baseball is at its best when it is passed down from one generation to the next.